Mary Moody is a prolific gardening author and a presenter on ABC TV's 'Gardening Australia'. Her books include *The Good Life* (1995) and *A Gardener's Companion* (2001). Every year Mary leads treks to the Himalayas and other parts of the world to observe native flora. She lives in the Blue Mountains, New South Wales.

Au Revoir

Au Revoir
MARY MOODY

MACMILLAN

Pan Macmillan Australia

First published 2001 in Macmillan by Pan Macmillan Australia Pty Ltd
St Martins Tower, 31 Market Street, Sydney

Reprinted 2001, 2002 (three times), 2003 (three times),

National Library of Australia
Cataloguing-in-Publication Data:

Moody, Mary.
Au revoir.

ISBN 0 7329 1109 5.

1. Moody, Mary – Homes and haunts – France. 2. Solitude.
3. Women – Australia – Biography. 4. France – Social life
and customs. I. Title.

155.92

Typeset in 11.5 pt New Baskerville by Midland Typesetters
Printed in Australia by McPherson's Printing Group
Cover and text design by Liz Seymour

To David Barwick and Emma Veitch-Turkington
who both loved this little corner of France

THE YEAR MY MOTHER TURNED FIFTY she had a nervous breakdown. My father had run off with another woman and Mum wrapped herself in a blanket of sleeping tablets and alcohol. She lost her high-profile job as the public relations executive for an international cosmetics company. Her half century culminated in two dramatic attempts at suicide which were clinically treated, quite alarmingly, with several large doses of LSD. She never worked again.

The year of my mother's breakdown I turned twenty and I tried, with little compassion, to grasp the implications of her illness. After many years of my father's infidelity, heavy drinking and domestic violence, my love and respect for him had totally evaporated. From my point of view my mother was well shot of him. Being so young I was unable to come to terms with the notion that people of my parents' advanced age could still feel such intense love and passion that it could drive them to heights of rage and despair. My parents' behaviour simply appalled me. I did my best to escape by running away from home with an unsuitable long-haired local boy to enjoy the tail end of the swinging sixties. For me life was full of exciting possibilities—living in a share house in trendy Paddington, going to rock festivals, partying all night and working by day as a cadet journalist on a popular women's magazine. I became deeply resentful at having to spend so much of that year rescuing my mother from her ongoing crisis. I ran out of patience with ambulance dashes to hospital casualty departments and visits to the weird psychiatric clinic where she was being treated.

At fifty, the women of my mother's generation were considered old. For many, after their fiftieth birthday celebrations it was downhill all the way. Middle age meant blue rinses and tight perms and Friday nights at the bingo. From my self-obsessed, youthful perspective I believed that my mother should just pull herself together, forget about her failed marriage and get on with growing old gracefully.

The year I turned fifty it dawned on me that I was exactly the same age my mother had been when I'd thought she had 'stopped living'. Suddenly, and with some guilt, I saw clearly for the first time how my mother must have been feeling that terrible year. My own life had taken a very different path from hers—I had a solid marriage, financial security, a busy and successful career and a wonderful collection of children and grandchildren. I was happy but also very aware that for my generation fifty is still considered quite young. Sexy, even. Certainly not the beginning of the end. While my mother at fifty could see no further than the black hole created by my father's departure, I saw my life as only just starting in so many ways. Instead of feeling pain and despair, I was feeling joy and excitement.

The year I turned fifty, in memory of my mother, I decided to claim six months for myself. I abandoned my career, my husband, my children and grandchildren, my friends, my home and my large garden, and went on a journey alone, to find myself.

1

I AM A CLASSIC BABY boomer. I was born into relative affluence and, like so many women of my generation, I've had it all. I have maintained a busy life and have worked professionally with virtually no time off for thirty years, while simultaneously rearing a larger than average family, balancing a relationship with my partner, managing a house, establishing a garden and generally being all things to all people. The expectations placed on us fifties girls have been enormous, and many have crumbled under the strain, admitting that being superwoman just isn't worth it. I somehow managed to survive, but—oddly enough—only with considerable help from my mother.

My mother regained her mental health, but really only completely recovered following the death of my father, two years after the dramatic dissolution of their marriage. She moved to a wheat farm in northern NSW with my much older half-brother Jon, but within twelve months had injured her leg so badly in a fall that she needed total bed rest to recuperate fully. It was harvest time and Jon simply couldn't cope, so Mum arrived on our doorstep to stay for three weeks. Somehow this turned into twenty-three years. My husband used to joke that it was like the mythical aunt who comes to dinner and never leaves, but somehow for all of us it seemed just right. By this stage we had two small children. Living up north, Mum had sorely missed them, and I had certainly missed having her around during those busy years with a young family. My relationship with her, which had been greatly strained during the years of her marriage breakup and nervous breakdown, was miraculously healed at the birth of my first child. It was quite amazing how her spirits lifted when this small wrinkled person arrived on the scene. She even wrote me a long and apologetic letter acknowledging how bad things had been, and how having a grandchild had somehow changed her life. Suddenly she was more positive, she had something to live for again. With her shock of unruly grey hair, her sharp wit and her irreverent sense of humour, she obviously had a huge impact on our lives over such a long period. She maintained her penchant for whisky and cigarettes, carefully eyeing the clock every evening for the stroke of five, when the lid would come off the bottle. But her contribution to our family life greatly outweighed her long-acquired bad habits.

My partner of nearly thirty years is a filmmaker, eleven years my senior. David and I got together in 1972 when I was working as a publicist for a commercial television station in Sydney where he was in production with a television series. The first time I saw David walking along the gloomy corridors near my office I was aghast: he was a bear-like man in his early thirties, balding on top but with blond-streaked hair at the back and sides that swept

4

down over his shoulders—and he had a brilliant red beard that came close to reaching his belt buckle.

'There's a man who works at the station,' I reported to Mum that weekend, 'who looks very much like an oversized garden gnome.'

Not long separated from his first wife Kathleen, and still on the rebound from a disastrous affair with a pretty young woman in the production office, David really shouldn't have been all that interested in entering into another full-on relationship. Yet he pursued me quite obsessively, and within a few months of meeting him we started living together. One of the first questions David posed to me in those early months of our relationship concerned having a child together. He already had a son, Tony, who had been born not long after the split-up with Kathleen, and he felt very distanced from him. David seemed desperate to have a child and for reasons I still cannot begin to fathom, I cheerfully fell in with the idea. I have often wondered why I was so compliant, given that it could easily have been a recipe for disaster: my youth and background of emotional turmoil combined with his poor history of relationships. I don't remember thinking it through for a moment, or trying to analyse the pros and cons. I simply stopped taking the pill and we produced our first child—a daughter, Miriam—in 1973. Two years later we followed with a son, Aaron, and not long after, with Mum in tow, we moved the entire household to the Blue Mountains, two hours west of Sydney.

As a flower child of the sixties I felt passionately that my children should grow up surrounded by pollution-free green fields, eating nothing but organic, home-grown fruit and vegetables. However I also had a fairly well-developed work ethic and couldn't see myself floating around a free-love commune or living completely off the land. The compromise was a house and large garden in the mountains where I could work as a freelance writer and still give our children a healthy lifestyle, plus all the home-grown vegetables I could force down their throats. It was here that I taught myself to garden. I quickly discovered it was more than just a practical acquisition. It was a passion.

In 1980 our second son, Ethan, was born in the front room with a midwife, neighbours, pet dog and older children in attendance. By this time David's son Tony, now aged eight, was also living with us, so we were a large and boisterous family of seven. I would have happily continued producing babies as I adored being pregnant and giving birth, but David had financial reservations about supporting such a large tribe. I rather reluctantly undertook surgery to halt my fertility. It occurred to me then—and has often since—that as it was his desire that the baby-making finish, it should have been him to brave the surgeon's knife.

During these years when the children were young I continued working as a freelance journalist and author, an ideal career for a young mother because it meant I could basically work from home. In the beginning developing the disciplines necessary to juggle a busy family life with magazine and publishing deadlines wasn't easy, but my sense of survival took over. I quickly discovered that if I didn't work consistently or if I left everything to the last moment (as most journalists inevitably do) life deteriorated into a nightmare. The secret was good organisation and an ability to cope with long days. I usually started early by taking some time in the garden before getting the kids up for school. I worked in the morning, shopped, cooked and did housework in the afternoon and tried to knock off for a beer and to start cooking dinner by five in the evening. We had a wide circle of good friends and although we were often fairly broke, these years were really the best for us. David was away an awful lot during that time. For almost twenty years he spent the greater part of each week at his office in the city; then, when actually filming, he would be away for weeks or even months at a time.

Being an independent producer in the Australian film industry is not the most financially secure of professions. We were often anxious about when the next bundle of money would come or where it would come from. So it was essential for me to keep working steadily as a backstop to the ups and downs of David's career. The saving grace was having my mother around for company and support; without her the lonely evenings after the children had gone to bed would have driven me mad. Mum had a fine mind and a wonderful, wicked way of handling people. She passionately followed the daily news in the papers, on the radio and television, having herself trained as a journalist. She read voraciously, was devoted to her grand-children, loved to cook, and loved to help care for the animals: as well as dogs, cats, chickens and ducks, at times we also had guinea pigs, sheep, goats, rabbits and fish. Right up until her death at the age of seventy-six she could still take down shorthand at 140 wpm and do all the newspaper crosswords every morning. The only downside was Mum's increasing dependence on the bottle for nightly enjoyment, and the repeated falls she had of an evening weaving from bedroom to bathroom.

On the up side, David and I both loved our working lives and were constantly stimulated by our various independent writing and filmmaking projects. Our weekends were very lively indeed—always a loving reunion when David came home on Friday nights, followed by two days of lavish meals, entertaining, bush walks, open fires, good music and visitors from the city. It really was the good life.

In 1992, after twenty-one years of this happy cohabitation, David and I took the plunge and got married. It had taken us this long even to think about marriage because David and his previous wife Kathleen had never actually organised a divorce, even after more than two decades of separation. They did start proceedings twenty-odd years earlier, but David so infuriated the sitting judge by debating with him the informal arrangements that he and Kathleen had made for the care of Tony, that the case was subsequently thrown out of court. So they remained legally bound for the entire time we had been together producing our large family.

Although I publicly avowed that getting married was just a good excuse for a party, in truth it was the formalising of the commitment we had made so many years before. Our wedding ceremony, which was meant to be a brief prelude to a sumptuous Italian feast began by being slightly comical, then rapidly degenerated into a farce. The celebrant decided the occasion was deeply romantic, and therefore deserving of much handclasping, teary eyes and poetry reading. I had never intended it to be like this, indeed I loathe overly sentimentalised ceremonies of any description. I carefully prepared the celebrant with some succinct words we had written, explaining to her that we were already quite an old 'married couple'; in spite of this, she insisted on treating us like a pair of eighteen-year-old star-crossed lovers. I couldn't make eye contact with David for fear of dissolving into hysterics, and one glance at our now almost-adult children revealed that they were finding the whole thing more than a little embarrassing. I am convinced that most marriage celebrants are frustrated actors who relish the opportunity to overact their socks off. But it provided plenty of laughs during the six-hour-long lunch, and we certainly didn't forget the occasion in a hurry.

By the mid 1990s Tony, Miriam and Aaron had started leaving home to pursue their various educational options. Although life became easier with just one teenager at home, my career suddenly became extremely busy and demanding, with television segments to film and monthly magazine deadlines to meet, as well as book contracts. About this time my mother's health started to deteriorate. She didn't like being left alone in the house, which meant we had to make sure there was always someone around to keep a watchful eye on her. If I was away filming, one of the children would come home and stay with her; sometimes it would even be one of their friends, as she had attracted a large retinue of young followers who had adopted her as their surrogate grandma.

Then a strange thing happened. Miriam, who was in her final year of university, announced that she and her boyfriend Rick were going to have a baby. Before our youngest child had finished school David and I were going to be grandparents. Whatever happened to those years in between when we could enjoy having paid off the mortgage and have some peace and quiet? Have some time to ourselves without babies and high-chairs and bathtoys?

Yet becoming a grandmother, I quickly discovered, was one of the sweetest joys of my life. Miriam had watched with fascination while her young brother Ethan was being born at home; now in turn she opted for a homebirth in the small townhouse she and Rick shared a few kilometres from her university in Canberra. Seemingly without effort, she gave birth to Eamonn in May and completed her degree at the end of that year.

Our lives changed dramatically in the next few years. Mum died suddenly of a ruptured aorta—attributed directly to her heavy smoking. During her last two years she had been extremely frail and had had numerous falls. Fortunately the impact of most of these was softened by her state of inebriation. She seemed half pickled most of the time, although I only ever saw her drinking in the evenings. Yet throughout those last few years her spirit and sharp mind never diminished, so her sudden death caused us all a great deal of shock and grief. But there were happy changes too. During this period Miriam married Rick and they moved back to the mountains where they subsequently gave birth to two more sons, Sam and Theo. Aaron and his girlfriend Lorna, not to be outdone, produced their baby, Hamish, about the same time as Sam was born. Four grandsons in five years. Quite a surprise for someone not yet fifty.

For years I had dreamed and fantasised about living overseas for a period of time—perhaps for a whole year. Although David—in the course of his film-making—had done much more travelling than I had, during the past decade I managed to squeeze in several forays into Europe, the UK and America, mainly to photograph beautiful gardens for my pictorial library. In our travels together David and I particularly loved Ireland, Italy and France. We often talked about the possibility of dropping out for while and living abroad. Financially it always seemed just out of reach, and now that our lives were filled with small grandchildren, the idea of escaping seemed even further from reality.

Suddenly, with my fiftieth year looming I decide to take some affirmative action on my own behalf. I will take six months and spend it alone. I decide to go to France. It seems the most comfortable and the most affordable option. And David and I have always loved being there, whether it is Paris, or the Loire Valley, Normandy or Provence.

While I am not feeling unduly stressed or dissatisfied with my life, I am beginning to ponder a few simple truths. I realise I have never lived alone and that for most of my life I have lived under the same roof as my mother. I have needed to work from the day I left school—through pregnancies and babies and child rearing—and my working life has escalated into a series of hectic deadlines and pressures and high expectations. I have been, for almost twenty years, the primary carer for our children, with David away so much of the time. I am a grandmother and a mother simultaneously, the two stages of my life having merged into one. More importantly, I realise that I have never had time in my life to stop and think. To be reckless or irresponsible or just plain lazy. Perhaps to sleep in or to spend the whole day in bed without actually being sick. To wake up in the morning and wonder *What will I do today?* , then to roll over and go back to sleep.

I realise that for many, many people at my stage of life, both men and women, the idea of stopping and dropping out for a bit is simply not possible. For me it will be difficult, but I am determined to make it happen.

It is time to let go.

2

IF YOUR PARENTS AND the circumstances of your child-hood shape you as an adult, then I certainly must be the product of mine. I can only believe that my person-ality and my character strengths and weaknesses were forged during a growing-up period that was a bit of a roller coaster, bouncing along with many highs and lows. Now, as a woman of nearly fifty, I am aware that my childhood memories and sen-sations were both good and bad. The setting was certainly one of the really good things. The Sydney harbour suburb of Mosman during the 1950s and 60s was a heavenly place to grow up, both for its physical beauty and for the safety and freedom allowed children during those innocent years. Once you learned how to swim out of your depth, the beach became yours to explore without adult supervision. There were plenty of safe places away from the sharks—a sweeping netted area, a small but crystal-clear rockpool, and the baths—as well as rocky headlands to explore, massive fig trees along the Esplanade to climb and glori-ously clean stretches of sand that were seldom crowded. At times my brother Dan and I had Balmoral beach entirely to ourselves. We knew every rockpool and channel and understood the best times to swim according to the tides. The only danger was the summer sun which scorched our fair and freckled skins, creating the embryo cancers that decades later we are having frozen from our hands, cheeks and foreheads.

We lived in a small second-floor apartment in a block of liver brick flats with fantastic views out to the headlands that opened into Sydney harbour. Our parents were both journalists and our mother Muriel, having been brought up in what she considered the stigmatised working-class western suburb of Haberfield, had chosen Mosman as a suitable suburb for the family. Ironically, these days Haberfield and its surrounding suburbs are considered trendy, with the Federation-style brick houses that she so detested now fetching vast prices for their proximity to the city and their yuppie desirability.

Our father, Theo, came from the slums of Fitzroy in Melbourne where he had helped support his mother and family after the early death of his solicitor father from syphilis and alcoholism. Theo was born in 1910, the fourth child in a family of four brothers and one sister. They lived over a pawn shop and my father claimed there was a pub on every corner. In later life he attributed his extreme fondness for alcohol to this, but it was much more likely due to the dodgy genetic inheritance from his father.

Theo had left school at fourteen and was largely self-educated. I have no idea what menial jobs he took to survive during his early teens but I know—from his occasional half-sloshed reminiscences—that he devoured knowledge through his love of reading and by the age of twenty was both literate and confident enough to gain a cadetship on one of the Melbourne daily newspapers. His voracious reading included the wordy volumes of Karl Marx, Engels and Lenin, and their philosophies, combined with the human deprivations of the Great Depression, filled my father with a great passion for social justice. He joined the Communist Party in Melbourne in the early 1930s and remained a card-carrying member until his death in 1972.

Theo's first marriage at the age of twenty-one was to the young and beautiful Veronica Fanning. Her family were respectable and financially successful members of the Victorian Catholic establishment, and her father was later to become the Postmaster General of Victoria. Veronica's family were horrified at her liaison with Theo so in order to get married the young couple eloped, travelling as far away as London to escape her family disapproval. In England my older siblings, Jonathan and Margaret, were born, but lack of work brought the young family back to Australia, where my father got a job as a reporter on a Sydney newspaper.

Various aspects of Theo's personality began to emerge even at this early age. He drank heavily and spent a good proportion of his wages on elegant clothing for himself, frittering away the remainder on horse racing and womanising. He often worked the night shift and came home drunk in the early hours of the morning. Veronica was in constant despair. One morning he came home and found she had committed suicide, leaving him with two children under the age of ten. Various family members rallied to his aid, but it didn't take Theo long to find and fall in love with my mother. Ten years his junior, Muriel Angel was working as court reporter and copytaker on the *Daily Telegraph* where Theo was news editor at the time. Muriel came from a large family of journalists and was considered a great beauty in the Celtic tradition, with a mane of jet black hair and bright blue eyes. Even then she was painfully thin from her habit of chain-smoking instead of eating. Her father had also been a court reporter and a freelance journalist and, like so many in his profession, was a problem drinker who failed to provide very well for his family. Given this, why our mother was attracted to our hard-drinking, self-centred father is hard to comprehend, although from photographs Theo was undoubtedly handsome and dashing, with a head of springy bright red curls. He also had a wicked sense of humour. This humour—and his hair—are part of my inheritance.

Despite her youth, Muriel was more than up to the task of taking on two young and obviously damaged children. The new family immediately got along famously, which was just as well: within weeks of getting married, my father was posted to New York as a war correspondent for the *Daily Telegraph*, and he left Muriel alone in Sydney with the children. It took a year before she and the children were able to join him, and their time together in America was, I feel certain, the happiest of their married life.

3

FOR MANY YEARS DAVID and I had contemplated the idea of taking a year off work and spending it living somewhere overseas. It's the usual sort of dream for people who have travelled, especially if they fall in love with a particular country or region and yearn for a more leisurely stay. In our various travels over the years we have discussed spending more time in the Italian countryside, probably Umbria; in rural Ireland, possibly south of Dublin; and in the south of France, undoubtedly Provence.

I start by making plans for a break of six months—that's all we can afford—from the end of May until December. David has been talking about spending at least part of the time travelling with me, but then two film projects he has been working on for years suddenly look like going ahead, which means that he will need to be in Queensland filming during that period. I am determined to go away regardless, and notify the ABC of my intentions. The television program I work on is popular and rates well with the audience, but in my opinion it has become rather stale over the last few years; my going away will give the producers an opportunity to try some new faces and perhaps shake up the format a little. In my heart of hearts I would like to move on. After nine years with the program I feel a bit lacking in inspiration (not to mention frustration after years of dealing with some of the mediocre executives at the ABC). But I know it's not a good idea to shut the door completely as no doubt I'll be desperate for some sort of regular income when I return.

Every year I lead a trek to the Himalayas in India during late May. My plan after this is to fly from Delhi to Paris then on to Nice. The Indian trek takes groups to look at the flora of the Harki Dun Valley in a glorious eight-day climb high into the mountains in the northern part of India. I am the group leader, but we also take a local botanist and one or two highly experienced local guides, as well as the ubiquitous porters. This trek has become one of the most enjoyable and exciting sidelines of my work, and I look forward to it every year with pleasure.

My original plan is to find a place to live near Grasse in Provence, a region we have visited several times after attending the Cannes Film Festival, and where we have come to love the atmosphere and the countryside. However my Grasse real estate agent contacts have been finding it difficult to get low-cost accommodation for six months—the summer period is always booked out and rentals are at a premium. All they can offer is a fifth floor apartment in a modern block on the outskirts of the township. This is far from the romantic garret in which I picture myself. I love the old stone houses and the narrow, winding back streets and would prefer to rent a simple room or two above a shop or in any old building. I want peeling shutters and creaky stairs and I don't care if the bathroom and kitchen are basic, as long as I have a bed and table and chair. But organising such a modest wish list from the other side of the world is difficult, and I am beginning to think I will never find a place to stay.

Then my friend Gil Appleton suggests I contact an old boyfriend of hers from the seventies, Jock Veitch, a retired journalist now living in the tiny village of St Caprais in a little-known rural region in France called the Lot. It's certainly a long way from my first choice of Provence, being close to the Spanish border in the southwest, a region which David and I have only ever driven through, but it might just be worth a try. I email Jock, introduce myself, and ask if he knows of any rental accommodation in his region. He says he'll ask around and over the next few weeks I get a couple of tentative replies from him, but nothing definite. Then he writes and offers me a room in his house until I can find what I am looking for. This takes quite a weight off my shoulders and I happily accept his offer of a roof over my head. I really know very little about the region, but it's rural, it's remote and it's French, and that's good enough for me.

I haven't really allocated a financial budget for this trip, but I will have to do it as cheaply as possible. Living overseas, it's easy to spend hundreds, even thousands, of dollars a week on rent, and hundreds more to hire a car, not to mention living expenses. As I am without an income for six months I can't justify spending up big time. This isn't a junket and isn't going to be a rich woman's retreat. I don't want to do it as rough and ready as a young backpacker, but neither do I want to drain the family coffers in the process. My needs are fairly simple and surely part of the enjoyment will come from living without all the clutter of modern life. I can cheerfully live without satellite TV as long as

I have a radio and can find a local channel that plays good music. I don't need a swimming pool or a sun deck as long as there are rivers to walk beside and sunny places to curl up with a book.

Knowing that I can land on Jock's doorstep gives me confidence to proceed with my plans. I organise to borrow a car for the six months from our old friends Richard and Fabienne Barnes, who live in Nice; the mobility will be important for me. I spend a lot of time daydreaming about the trip, picturing myself in cafés and wandering down country lanes. But I am also feeling very pressured about organising the logistics, as well as tying up all the loose ends of my professional and private life so that I can actually get on the plane with some peace of mind.

4

 MY MOTHER MURIEL WAS A spirited and warm hearted young woman who loved reading, walking and classical music. She had been a promising ballet dancer in her early teens but, like our father, her family circumstances dictated that she leave school and abandon her ballet studies in order to work and help contribute financially. In those days there were no pensions for widows as such, and everyone needed to rally to support relatives who were unable to work.

My brother Dan and I were not born until after the war when Muriel and Theo returned from their exciting years abroad. Having been unable to conceive during the entire time they lived in America, Mum saw a gynaecologist once back in Sydney; after a simple curette, she produced three babies in three and a half years. First Daniel, then me and twelve months later baby Jane, who died towards the end of her first year of life. This sudden population explosion placed a huge strain on the family, with two teenagers and three babies in what was only a two-bedroom flat on the second floor. The dark and dreary laundry was in the basement and consisted of a gas-heated copper and manual wringer; steaming hot clothes were handled with a wooden pole, and after wringing were hung out on a bowed line lifted high with a wooden clothes prop. Somehow my mother managed to wash our clothes, including dozens of nappies every day, and keep the family fed in spite of the difficult circumstances. We had no car and the shops were at the top of an extremely steep hill. My father didn't help very much domestically—apart from buying a loaf of fresh bread every evening at Circular Quay on his way home from work.

When Jane became ill and was taken to the Children's Hospital, things became really grim for the family, though my information on this period is largely based on my mother's later recollections. She was not encouraged to visit Jane—in those days parents were considered a nuisance by the hospital staff—and in any event the hospital was in Camperdown, a good two- or three-hour journey on public transport from Balmoral Beach. No clear diagnosis was ever given, and Jane simply lost condition over a period of six months. She never came home again.

What happened during this period set the scene for what was to become the dark side of my childhood. Both our parents began drinking heavily and fighting violently on a regular basis. Their reminiscences of their time in America included constant references to drinking—it was the fashion to drink spirits in vast quantities during the war period, especially among journalists and people in the creative and artistic professions. Mum often recounted stories of drunken binges first in New York, later in their clapboard house in Connecticut. They fell in with a wealthy, hard-drinking crowd and many of the photographs from that time, although glamorous, reveal puffy faces and glassy eyes.

The habits formed during these first years of their marriage remained with them both for the rest of their lives. They also smoked heavily and although Mum didn't generally start drinking until the evening, she could down a large bottle of sherry or the best part of a bottle of whisky in just a few hours. Dad started drinking early in the day. On his way to work, at around eight o'clock in the morning, he would have two 'heart starters' at the Ship Inn, an early opener at Circular Quay. At work, he would leave his desk on the hour and go downstairs into Castlereagh Street to have two drinks at the corner pub. Surprisingly, he didn't frequent the bar during his lunch hour, but spent the time lifting weights at the gymnasium of the fashionable City Tattersalls Club. He was vain about his appearance, and wanted to look fit and flat-tummied in spite of his dissipated lifestyle. He had also continued his habit of engaging in torrid love affairs, and obviously believed he needed to look good to attract suitable women.

Mum, stuck at home with two toddlers, grieving for baby Jane, and knowing of my father's constant dalliances with younger, available women, drank even more heavily than she had done before. Jonathan escaped by qualifying as a marine engineer, which allowed him to spend most of his time at sea and return for just a few weeks at a time. Margaret was in the final year of a fine arts degree at East Sydney Tech, which infuriated my father whose political ideologies regarded the arts as unnecessarily frivolous and bourgeois. He was continuing to wave the red flag of communism in total contradiction to his own self-indulgent way of life. He and Margaret clashed badly. She was a powerfully intelligent young woman who always stood up to him, often defending my mother and digging her heels in during repeated confrontations. Eventually, after a particularly ugly fight on her eighteenth birthday, she stormed out and never returned. She contacted Mum once or twice but within a few years emigrated to Canada where she became an arts academic.

Margaret's sudden disappearance from our lives had a profound impact on me. I feel certain she must have been the primary carer for Dan and me during the period when our sister Jane was dying. I often lay in bed at night, listening to my parents brawling in the living room, and fantasising that Margaret would suddenly walk back through the door and rescue me. It never happened. I dreamt of her vividly for decades.

I still feel very sad about having lost my sister from my life and carry around a hope that I will track her down one day, if she is still alive. I have tried using the Internet to trace her through various universities in Canada where I believe she worked during the seventies and eighties, but I have yet to have any success. My brother Jon, on the other hand, who eventually retired from the sea and moved to northern New South Wales, has remained very close to the family.

During the early years of our childhood the small flat was often alive with visitors, indulging in marathon drinking sessions and stimulating debates and discussions. Those who visited were virtually all members of the Communist Party, and they included writers and artists such as Judah Waten, Frank Hardy and Noel Counhihan. Great ideas were discussed but sometimes the parties would deteriorate into squabbles or worse. Theo's drinking would get the better of him and he would become extremely argumentative and aggressive. His personality was such a mystery to me as a child. I was generally very frightened of him, and always intimidated. When sober (which was rare) he was a charming and self-effacing man with a gentle warmth. When slightly in his cups (which was for most of the day) he continued to be most affable. All the people who worked with him—especially the women—had a high regard for him both professionally and as a 'good' man. He was much loved at Consolidated Press where he worked for nearly thirty years. It was at night, when he relaxed and drank ferociously, that he could turn nasty. On many evenings he would simply drink straight from his flagon of claret and fall into bed early to sleep off his excesses. However if my mother started needling him, as so often she did, things could and would rapidly deteriorate.

The lack of money was a major source of tension between our parents. Dad was on a comparatively high wage for those days—for many years he had a margin above a super A grade, which was the maximum amount a journalist could be paid—but he had never learned to handle money, and was especially extravagant in relation to himself. He continued to spend a lot on his own clothes, shopping at the best menswear stores in the city, and he always looked elegant as he left for the *Telegraph* offices in the morning. In heated rows with my mother he rationalised that his position demanded he be well turned out, while she was still wearing the remnants of clothes she brought back from New York almost a decade before. He spent a large percentage of his income on tobacco and alcohol and gambled weekly on the telephone with an SP bookie. Considering his frame of mind most Saturday evenings, I guess he seldom won any of these bets on the races. He loved food and often lunched during the week at Sydney's then fashionable restaurants such as The Greeks and Romanos. His other passion of course was young women—who

were probably the reason he was often dining out at lunchtime—
and his constant love affairs were also a drain on our finances.
We never actually went hungry, because he at least gave my
mother housekeeping money every pay day (or perhaps she
wrestled it out of him) but that was the only cash she ever saw.

When things were tight Dad simply shoved bills into drawers
and forgot about them. He considered electricity accounts and
even the monthly rental on the apartment to be somehow
beneath him. Bailiffs occasionally came to the door early
Saturday morning demanding money for various unpaid bills,
and this ensured that the rest of the weekend was a nightmare of
screaming and shouting. Sometimes the fights would escalate
into violence. I remember vividly lying in bed and hearing my
mother's body slam into the living room wall. Although much
smaller than him and very thin, she would also attack him and
this would make him even more deranged. Once he threw her
down the front stairs of the flats and she slept in the car. I lay
awake for hours, waiting for the fight to restart, but all went
quiet. When I got up the next morning they were cuddling in
bed together and apologised for the scene of the night before:
it was the only time they ever did.

Naturally the neighbours complained and sometimes the
police were called. Even as a child I felt that the family was under
siege: my mother would try and sneak up the back stairs to avoid
bumping into the neighbours, as she suffered greatly from a
sense of shame at what was happening. Her own father's
drinking had never been openly acknowledged by her family, so
when he was drunk he was 'sick', and when he was out of work
it was always someone else's fault. This tendency to blame an
external cause for every personal failing was very big in my

family. My mother constantly reassured me, during quiet moments when they were getting along well together, that my father's drinking and bad temper was the result of his sad life. His struggle. Veronica's death. Jane's death. There was always a good reason.

From sheer necessity Mum went out and got a job during a period when mothers with young children simply did not work outside the home. In 1957 she was fortunate to find a position in the relatively new field of public relations, for a charitable organisation based in Mosman; it was ideal for her, being part-time and quite well paid. Suddenly she had new clothes and smart shoes and was able to visit the hairdresser. She even saved up and bought a car and the new mobility transformed her life. Soon there was a washing machine and a new fridge. Eventually there was a television. And a lot of the strain went out of the marriage.

PEOPLE SENSIBLE ENOUGH TO lead simple lives can pack
their bags two days before they leave on holidays, turn
off the electricity and lock the front door. My life has
become so complex that escaping for three weeks entails at least
a month of frantic preparations and it follows that escaping for
six months will bring on a mind boggling list of tasks to be
accomplished. I can withdraw from my television filming for
the entire period, however I have to complete some last-minute
filming for two documentaries, one local and one international,
about the landscaping for the Olympic Games. We have been
progressively filming the progress of the landscape for more
than four years, and the completion of the project involves
previewing all the existing material, editing out unnecessary
sequences and writing a master script that will link all the various
segments together into an integrated overview of how the
landscape was accomplished. Plus there's two or three days
filming, on top of my usual schedule.

I have also been asked to continue my monthly magazine

articles, and I decide to write these in advance, so that I don't even have to think about them, let alone meet deadlines during my break. This involves preparing six separate articles, compiling photographs, captions and the smaller columns and items that are part of the publishing contract. I am also approached to put together a glossy magazine on Australian wildflowers targeted at the Olympic visitors—it must look totally scrumptious with more photographs than words. The extra money will certainly come in handy, but there is a lot of organisation involved, not to mention tracking down suitable photographs. Added to this is the ongoing editorial work for a large gardening book, which I have written the previous year and which is now in production. I have to work with the editor to make changes and corrections, adding where necessary and cutting back repetitive entries. This work is normally stretched over six months and I am compressing it into six weeks.

I also need to prepare myself physically for the Indian trek, which is quite demanding. Early every morning, I put on my walking boots and drive to Wentworth Falls where I make a mad dash to the head of the waterfall and back, trying to reduce the time it takes every day. On the way up my heart thumps wildly and I struggle for breath against the cold early morning air, and on the way down my knees jar at the impact with the rocks. These are exactly the sort of conditions I will be facing in the Himalayas—rocky, uneven steps, some very steep climbs and altitude. It takes less than forty-five minutes there and back, but it's just one more thing to accomplish every day before I leave.

I need to organise two visas, one for India and one for France. The Indian visa is very straightforward, just a formality, but the French long stay visa quickly becomes a nightmare. Australians visiting France for less than three months do not require a visa at all, but if a visitor wants to dally longer the bureaucracy imposes a maze of requirements. I should have realistically allowed at least four months to get through all the paperwork that acquiring a long stay French visa involves. Firstly I need to have my fingerprints taken at the local police station and then provide a document from the NSW Police Department verifying that I have no criminal record. Fingerprinting techniques have obviously not kept up with the digital age, and I leave Katoomba Police Station covered to the wrists with smears of thick black ink, regretting I chose to wear a cream jacket on that particular day. I then have to visit a doctor—one nominated by the French Consulate—for a routine medical examination. The doctor is French, naturally, and lives in Sydney, so a whole day is required for travelling. He wants to know what my parents died from, and I am reluctant to admit excessive alcohol consumption— although, in hindsight, I wonder if this may have had little negative reaction from the wine-obsessed French. I am relieved that his methods are not like the French doctor I once visited while at the Cannes Film Festival, who required me to strip naked and lie on a leather couch (with mood lighting) while he checked me for an ear infection. This doctor is so elderly that I feel certain he has forgotten what a naked woman looks like. Or at least I hope he has.

I am also required to furnish a statutory declaration stating that I will not attempt to find work in France; banking records to prove that I can financially support myself for six months; and proof of complete and up-to-date medical and travel insurance. The most tricky requirement, however, is a letter from a French resident stating that he or she will be responsible for my accommodation by providing an address that will be known to the government. My friends near Nice, Richard and Fabienne Barnes, who are lending me the car, can do this for me, but not without some considerable hassle. The letter must be signed at their local mairie, or town hall, and they in turn must produce all sorts of evidence to prove that they are suitable hosts for a reckless Australian woman—rental receipts, recent phone bill receipts, etc. It is a nightmare, both for them and for me. The days to my departure are ticking down, and the forms provided by the consulate lead me to believe that even after furnishing all this paperwork, it may take up to a month to process the visa. Luckily I develop a good telephone relationship with the young woman who is handling this area and she assures me that it can be pushed through quickly. Meanwhile Richard is away working on the other side of France, and hasn't been able to get his letter signed. I am desperate with anxiety. But finally it all comes together just a few days before I am scheduled to leave, having cost a small fortune in fees and charges, travel back and forth to Sydney, vital days for finishing off work lost to running around, and endless phone calls, faxes and emails between home and France. The long stay visa, however, looks most impressive in my passport; silver and embossed, it is in typical French good taste. The Indian visa—simply a smeared rubber stamp that has been initialled by some petty official—is very understated by comparison.

My main concern in being away so long is over my four grandsons. I have developed a very close relationship with each one individually, spending hours, sometimes days, with them every week. They stay the night on a rotating basis, and I cook meals during the week to give my daughter Miriam and my daughter-in-law Lorna a break at the end of the day. I remember clearly the tiredness that seeps in by late afternoon for a mother caring for a gaggle of toddlers, and I always had my mother around to help me. It's the least I can do to carry on the tradition, but apart from that, I love it. I have tried to structure my working life so that, excepting the periods when I am away filming, I can knock off work by mid afternoon and get involved in looking after the boys. I often pick Eamonn up from school, standing in the playground and chatting to the other mums just as I did twenty years ago with his own mother. I take them to swimming lessons and to the park but most of all I give them the free run of our house and large garden. They love collecting the eggs from the chickens and working in the vegetable garden, and I love having them underfoot. It's the physical relationship with young children that I find so satisfying: the spontaneous hugs and holding of hands, the rubbing down of their little pink bodies after a bath, the tickling and snuggling when they come into my bed at night.

Because of this closeness I know I must prepare them for my going away. For several months beforehand I talk about it casually. We look at the globe together to find France and India, we talk about how long six months is; to help the younger ones, who have no sense of time, to understand, I have nominated Christmas as the time when I will be back home with them all. They call me Mutie, because when Eamonn was born there were four great-grandmothers alive and kicking as well as two grandmothers and all the usual names—Grandma, Gran, Nana, Granny—were already taken. I tell them that Mutie will be having a lovely holiday in France then coming home in time for Christmas.

I am also concerned about the garden, though it is quite low
on my list of priorities. As I have been so frantically busy for
several months, it has already started falling into neglect and
without me around for such a long period it will no doubt run
riot. I film a segment for the program on how to prepare a
garden for a long absence; it's particularly aimed at all the
retired couples known as grey nomads who take off on caravan
holidays around Australia leaving their poor gardens to survive
alone for months, or even years. I smother everything with
newspaper and straw, install a few extra irrigation lines, and
prune back as much as possible. But it's all done in haste and I
simply have to banish it from my mind or it will drive me crazy.
I can always start again when I get back.

My four children grow quieter as the days grow closer to my
departure. They are thrilled for me, but also quite daunted at the
prospect of not having me around for such a long time. And
now, as an added emotional complication, Aaron and Lorna
announce that they are expecting their second child, which is
conceived after my decision to go and expected in early
September. I feel dreadful that I won't be around to help, having
been so closely involved in the births and aftermath of the other
four babies, but it's too late to change things. It will be good for
everyone having to cope without me being the constant
backstop. At least, I hope it will.

David has become rather withdrawn too, and anxious about
all the fine details and the logistics of travel. A natural worrier,
he is concerned with issues of safety such as driving in France,
and the fear of my getting lost. He is always the navigator and
international driver when we travel together, and I have always
cheerfully deferred in my role of passenger and bag carrier.

I think David is also contemplating that I might just be running away to find romance or to have an affair. After all, I was only twenty-one when we first got together and now I am nearly fifty. He hints at the possibility that I might have a fling. I laugh it off, of course, but it has occurred to me as well. I have always been far too busy being responsible and surrounded by too many people ever to engage in a clandestine affair. This could be my chance, and he knows it.

The day before I leave I should be packing, but so many last-minute things crop up to be attended to, and my bag sits empty in the corner of my room. We have a family farewell dinner which is unusually subdued, and in the morning I literally throw clothes into my pack at random. I must carry appropriate gear for trekking the Himalayas, including heavy boots and thermal underwear. There are countless emergency medications for this first part of the trip, and fortunately I had sorted them out weeks ago. I then need loose clothing for Delhi, which hovers around 45 degrees in May, and summer clothes for France. It will be winter by the time I leave, so I will also need a coat and gloves and warm pyjamas. I should have made a list, but without one I just hurl everything into the bag and hope for the best.

I thought I had said my final farewells to the family the previous night, but less than an hour before I am due to leave they start to arrive at the house, kids in tow. As David loads my bag and backpack into the car, I hug everyone tightly and they wish me a great journey. The little children have gone to play down in the back garden, and I wait until the last moment to say goodbye. Before I even get down to where they are gathering eggs I am sobbing like a fool. Eamonn, the oldest, is terribly embarrassed. He kisses me on the cheek and immediately turns back to what he was doing. At eighteen months, Theo is oblivious and Hamish, although just three, is too fascinated by his game to pay very much attention. However Sam, the sweet-natured, lisping one searches my red, tear-stained face with his soulful brown eyes.

'Why are you tho, tho thad, Mutie?' he asks.

'I'm not sad, Sam. I am happy. But I am going to miss you all very much.'

I dash to the gate, into the car, and continue to sob until we are way past Springwood. At the airport David and I share a drink with my closest friend Christine and her husband Richard. Our oldest son Tony and his wife Simone, who live in Sydney, also drop by for a last-minute hug. David has asked to have the last half hour alone, but we really have nothing much to say to each other. We sit in silence, glancing at the departure board as I sip my last Australian beer for quite some time. However, the look on his face when I push my bags through the customs gates says it all. It will be a rough six months for him, I am sure.

6

Growing up as the child of alcoholic parents in the 1950s was hard enough. Growing up as the child of communists during this repressive era made it even harder. For decades my father had managed to keep his political affiliations a secret from his employer, Sir Frank Packer, which enabled him to rise to the position of editor of the *Sunday Telegraph*; had Packer known my father was a card-carrying member of the Communist Party he would have been sacked on the spot. This meant that my father led a double life: by day he was the editor of a newspaper that espoused middle-class white Australian values, and at home he was a frustrated left-wing intellectual. To his credit, Packer rarely, if ever, interfered with the editorial content of the Sunday paper—even then it was considered more of a weekend entertainment paper than a hard-hitting news vehicle—unless, of course, there was a genuine news break in which case my father's basic journalistic instincts came to the fore. The only times Dad had a problem were late on Saturday night if Packer had lost heavily at the races and had too much to drink, when he could unexpectedly turn up and ask to see the first three pages. Usually this was okay, but every so often he would demand a remake or a rewrite, which really caused problems, especially if the paper was ready to go to press. Sunday mornings after such an event were fairly bleak in the Moody household.

At home my parents were determined that their children should follow their political beliefs. They took great pains to explain to us, in the most ridiculously simplistic terms, various aspects of communist doctrine, giving us catchphrases to quote to school friends about the evils of capitalism, and how the only hope for the future of humanity was if communism were to dominate the world. Despite the extremely anti-communist mood that prevailed during this period, my parents never warned us to keep our political beliefs under our hats and so, like an evangelist, I felt it was my duty to communicate these 'essential truths' to my school friends, even when I was very young. My brother Dan, less gullible and less gregarious than I, had the intelligence to work out pretty quickly that beating my parents' political drum would earn him few friends. I, on the other hand, found myself in endless debates and although I was never without a small handful of friends, I was treated with the utmost suspicion by most of my classmates.

Our indoctrination did not stop with politics. Religion was another favourite topic of derision. My parents taught me that religion was the means of keeping the masses oppressed and that therefore priests and ministers were evil people, probably child molesters, or at the very least sexually suspect. I was forbidden to attend a teenage girls' fellowship group organised by the local minister's wife. They were all lesbians according to my father, and I earnestly believed him without any understanding of the meaning of the word. It was hard fitting in with society when at home we were constantly told that all landlords, shopkeepers and police, and most politicians and people in any position of power or authority, were not only unintelligent but evil. As a result, for most of my childhood, I felt very much an outsider.

To balance this bleak view of the world, my parents somehow constructed an artificial picture of us as a perfect family. According to their version of our life, we were much brighter, better read and better looking than our peers and certainly the other families who lived in our neighbourhood. Their interpretation of our lifestyle led us to believe that we ate better food, had better jobs and were in fact superior in every way to those around us. I found this hard to reconcile against the reality of our unstable home life. Other people had cleaner houses and their parents spent a lot of time 'doing' things with them. Our flat was always a frightful mess and often very dirty because my mother had long ago abandoned all housework apart from the basics. Cleaning and tidying just were not on her agenda, and I was always too embarrassed to bring my friends home.

Part of my personality relished the fact that we were so different, so much apart from the crowd. Yet part of me longed to be ordinary, to be like everyone else. Until my mid teens I believed earnestly everything my parents told me, and my education as a budding young communist extended to being sent to a Eureka Youth League holiday training camp at Minto where we were given workshops on the glorious teachings of Marx and Lenin as well as singalongs around the campfire. It was just like the Boy Scouts and Girl Guides who, we were told, were subversive organisations aimed at indoctrinating young people to love God, Queen and Country. The hypocrisy was totally lost on me.

Despite the insanity during my childhood that stemmed directly from the relentless drinking and fighting, I never felt unloved or underprivileged. My parents were great talkers, they loved words and bandied them about to express their thoughts and ideas, both positive and negative. As a small child I remember my mother telling me constantly how much I was loved. I was reassured that I was very special and this certainly helped me to develop some self-esteem and confidence. However the atmosphere in the house had such a strong undercurrent of potential violence there was always a feeling of insecurity. At any moment there could be an irrational or unexpected explosion of anger. I seemed to spend my growing years constantly walking on eggshells, tiptoeing around and hoping that my father's temper would somehow remain under control. I realise now that even though he never once struck out at me directly, I was always terrified of his presence, anticipating his constant outbursts of anger.

And so the role I took on in my family was that of peacemaker. I tried to maintain some balance between my parents by being both extraordinarily helpful and compliant, as well as trying to be sweetly amusing. I developed all sorts of strategies for diffusing potentially explosive situations and lightening the atmosphere, and this method of managing people in awkward situations has remained with me all my life. I particularly tried to help my mother by doing things like tidying up the house and preparing the vegetables for the family meal before she arrived home from work. From the age of eight I was, without being asked, peeling potatoes and stringing beans and setting the table, so that all

Mum had to do was grill a few chops at the end of a busy working day. I became very good at seeing what needed to be done around the house, and then doing it without thought of complaint. My young mind must have worked out that if Mum was getting some assistance she would be less likely to nag at my father, and so the risk of an explosive argument would be reduced.

At school I adopted the role of class clown, using my rather underdeveloped wit and humour to draw attention to myself. This generally backfired, and I spent more than my fair share of time out of the classroom standing in the corridors, sometimes for an entire term thanks to my interjections and practical joking. My parents had little or no contact with the school and were quite unaware of my outrageous behaviour. In later years I even managed to intercept my school reports in the mail, and they somehow never even noticed that no end-of-year report had arrived. The main highlights at school were when I was asked to perform public speaking duties, or when my confident verbal skills made me a valued member of the debating team. Otherwise academically I just wasted my time, particularly at high school. And nobody at home was any the wiser.

Instilled in my heart from that period of my life is a terror of loud verbal or physical arguments. To this day I will walk twenty miles to avoid a confrontation, preferring instead to try and jolly people along rather than lock horns with them. I have a fear of uncontrolled anger, a fear it will escalate into violence, and I have always tried to keep a lid on such emotions within my own family. This need to please and to keep everybody feeling happy at all times stems directly from the way I learnt to cope with my parents at a very early age. There were so many unhappy people around me during those formative years that I resolved, quite unconsciously, to make sure that in my own family everybody would be happy ALL the time. A big ask. Certainly not very realistic.

Curiously I always craved my father's love and approval, despite the fact that as I grew older my love and respect for him greatly diminished. I tried to maintain contact, even after he abandoned my mother, and also tried to patch things up between them. Only once did I lose my cool: he returned for a week, bringing his clothes and other possessions, but sneaked back to his mistress again in the dead of night. It prolonged my mother's agony dreadfully. I went to the wardrobe where his immaculate and expensive clothes were folded in neat piles or hanging on quality wooden hangers, and chopped them into small pieces with my mother's sharp dressmaking scissors. Three or four suits, several tweed jackets, shirts, underwear and socks all felt my wrath. Neither he nor my mother ever said anything about it, it was as if it hadn't happened. Not long afterwards, my father committed suicide in the small, sordid flat that he had been sharing with the 'other' woman. I didn't cry at his funeral, and after the initial shock of his sudden departure abated, I barely gave him a passing thought.

7

TREKKING IN THE VEGETATION-RICH valleys of the Himalayas is one of the few perks of my television work
with the ABC. Travel companies frequently approach
television 'faces' to lead holiday tours overseas, and when I was
asked by an adventure travel company several years back to take
groups of Australian trekkers to look at alpine plants in northern
India, I eagerly jumped at the idea, and afterwards realised it
was something in my life that I found totally inspirational. After
my first trek I felt an exhilaration I had never experienced
before: I had accomplished a difficult climb to enter a rare and
exotic corner of the world seen by only a few adventurous individuals. Every year I am determined to repeat the sensation by
leading new groups of plant lovers into the wild mountains.

This year, however, my eagerness is tempered by something
else: I am itching to get to France. I arrive in Delhi late on a
Friday night, to a stifling heat. Even at night the city never
sleeps—teeming people, and traffic in all directions, shrill horns
honking, roadside vendors peddling spicy snacks, makeshift

cardboard and plastic dwellings flapping in the humid breeze. The next morning we catch the 6.15 train to Dehra Dun, in the foothills of the vast mountain ranges.

The train is packed and the journey itself is a bit of an adventure, with attendants rattling down the crowded corridors handing out hot tea, soft spicy omelettes and packets of sweets and biscuits. We reach Dehra Dun in the afternoon and take a bus for the long drive up winding mountain roads to the hill station of Mussoorie, which will be our first overnight stop. As we climb we can clearly see the filthy haze that lies over the plains stretching south, a combination of heat and pollution, and a normal feature of this part of the world where the intense summer heat of the flat country hits the cool mountain air. The views are breathtaking and the driving standard is hair-raising but I think that if you don't ever take a few risks in your life, you might as well stay home and watch the midday movie. And at the end of it will be this spectacular valley filled with brilliant flowers.

From Mussoorie, a British Raj town founded as a cool summer escape, we travel again by bus to Sankri, where the trekking finally begins. The climb itself takes four days, deep into the Har ki Dun valley. The uphill stretches are really hard work, but the winding paths, through woodlands and past primitive villages, are enchanting beyond belief, and the views from every aspect are truly mind boggling: soaring snow-capped mountains, deep valleys, cascades and waterfalls of icy water. As we tramp through forests of silver-trunked birches, stately cedars and fragrant pines, we seek out the unique flora we've primarily come for: wild Himalayan musk roses (*Rosa brunonii*); clumps of rare perennials including arisaemas with their metre-long, stick spadixes and majestic chequered fritillarias; carpets of blue and white anemones and dwarf iris; clumps of brilliant yellow marsh marigolds gathering beside every stream.

For me, this trek is a totally cleansing and purifying experience. To be without western food, including alcohol, for nearly two weeks somehow brings new life to my aging body. To be so far removed from any possibility of a telephone or a fax or an email is a calming feeling. To wake in the middle of the night and realise that you are completely separated from your 'real' world brings an exhilarating sense of freedom. Although slightly detached from reality, you are somehow more in touch with reality than ever before. It's a powerful sensation. I, for one, feel elated when we finally walk out of the last forest glen and into the quaint village of Taluka where hot tea is served in a smoky tearoom. My elation, I know, is partly due to the knowledge I'll soon be embarking on the next real adventure of this whole trip.

Back in Delhi, I prepare for France by jettisoning my trekking gear including day pack, heavy boots and thermal gear. I meet up with a fellow tour guide from the same company and he offers to take my gear back to Australia the following day. Alleviated of the trappings of my mountain adventure, I feel light and start to prepare myself mentally for my final escape from responsibility.

Before leaving India I do some last-minute shopping in the street bazaars and covered markets. Some presents for the children and grandchildren, and some gorgeous fabric which I intend using to make a patchwork quilt during my long evenings alone in France. The idea I have is to combine colours and designs from exotic India with peasant-style French fabrics into a bed cover that will, in many years to come, remind me of this lonely but unique journey I am taking. I select reds, oranges, yellows and blacks that I know will blend with the colours of rural France. With them safely tucked into my luggage, I head for the airport.

After the enormous effort of acquiring a long stay French visa, I am mortified at Paris when the airport immigration officials don't even bother to examine my passport. They merely wave me through the barrier with blank expressions. Why was I required to furnish such a complex array of legal documents vouching for my character and financial status when they are irrelevant to getting into the country? Theoretically I realise I can stay as long as I like: my passport hasn't even been stamped and therefore nobody will know on what date I arrived.

From Paris I take the domestic flight to Nice. Despite my pique over the visa, I immediately note with appreciation small cultural differences, like the casual acceptance of lap dogs at the airport. All around me perky heads are poking out from leather shoulder bags, bright eyes surveying the busy scene. Dogs are actually allowed to travel in the cabin with their owners, and in the window seat of the aisle opposite me a squash-faced Pekingese is sitting on his owner's lap watching the planes take off and land with intense interest. I wonder if the dog were a Labrador would it be allowed? Or a cat, for that matter.

On the plane I try listening hard and tuning my brain into conversations to get my ear working, but I realise I am not even picking up on the odd word. It's four years since I was last in France and obviously my grasp of the language is even more vague than I had hoped. This time I will make a concerted effort to speak and to listen and not just to use one or two words and lots of frantic hand actions to convey my meaning. Perhaps after six months I will be capable of a halting French conversation.

At Nice I am met by Fabienne, the wife of our old friend Richard Barnes. It's blazing hot and she takes me back to their cool and pretty apartment in Saint-Laurent-du-Var for icy drinks and a bowl of pasta. Fabienne is rare among French women in that she loathes cooking. Well, I think that she is rare, but she assures me that she's typical of her generation. She's incredibly slim too, so I imagine she doesn't enjoy eating much either—something soon confirmed when she picks at her food rather than eating with enthusiasm, unlike me. For many French women staying slim is a priority, in order to be able to wear the sort of clothes that convey a youthful image.

I have known Richard Barnes since he was twelve; he is the son of our dear old actor friend, Deryck Barnes, who lived at Sunny Corner near Bathurst. I didn't see much of Richard in his late teens, when he dropped out of university to the horror of his parents and went into commercial radio. In his early twenties, while on a working holiday in Europe with mates, he landed a job as an announcer on the English-speaking Radio Riviera in Monaco. He has been living in France ever since. Richard and Fabienne have two gorgeous daughters named in honour of the ships of Jacques Cousteau, Calypso and Océane.

Richard is generously lending me his old car for six months, which will be much cheaper and hopefully more reliable than buying an unknown car and selling it at the end of my trip. The car is a Peugeot 205 with a sunroof, considered by the French to be a bit of a classic, and very racy when I finally get to drive it. It has been garaged for eight months with a gear problem and the deal is that I pay for repairs, registration and insurance and it's mine until December. Unfortunately Richard has been very busy recently and he explains the car isn't quite ready. In fact it's far from ready with a smashed sunroof, defective tyres, and a faulty exhaust and muffler that make it sound like a rock-crushing machine. There's also paperwork to be done, and it looks as though I'll need to stay in Nice for at least the rest of the week until it's all in order.

I spend a few days exploring the waterfront villages around Nice, and also pay a courtesy visit to the elderly mother of a French friend who lives in Sydney. A widow close to eighty, Madame D'Erceville has no English and I have no French, yet she kindly invites me to lunch in her small apartment in Golfe Juan. I take the morning train with no problem, and when I arrive she greets me warmly. I have visited her on previous trips to France, but always in the company of a translator, so this will be a good test of my abilities to communicate. Mme D'Erceville has had several hip replacement operations and walks with some difficulty, but has managed to prepare a five-course meal which we eat accompanied by local wine. It's not long before my small repertoire of French phrases is exhausted and we lapse into a convivial silence. Over coffee she suggests I might like to see some television and I agree. She flicks on the set and quickly nods off to sleep while I sit and try to make some sense of the program, a foreign soapy badly dubbed into French. When she wakes I have another coffee and take my leave, determined to rectify my appalling lack of language.

While waiting for the car to be fixed I explore the shops for patchwork fabrics to blend in with the colourful selection I made in India. The cottons are beautiful, although quite expensive, and I buy some bright Provençal designs and some softer colours with the idea of making another small cot quilt for the grand-child who will be born while I am living in France. I am convinced that having a few sewing projects will help fill up the hours when I am alone, and prevent me from feeling too homesick.

By Friday the car is finally ready and I pack my gear and load up the boot. Richard offers to take me for a test drive and with great confidence I leap into the driver's seat and take off at speed. Of course the steering wheel, gears, controls and pedals are all on the opposite side of the car. I find it very difficult changing gears with my right hand, also to judge the distance from the centre line of the narrow streets that characterise most towns in France. My problem is not keeping to the right, but keeping too far over to the right so that the side mirror keeps banging into parked cars and traffic barriers. Richard screams in alarm when I nearly drive us into a ditch, he screams again when I narrowly miss sideswiping a van, and he shrieks in terror when I actually snap off the mirror on his side by hitting a barrier. I park outside his apartment and go in for coffee, my knees still knocking together in fright. Richard, though white as a sheet, cheerfully reassures me that all will be fine when I hit the open road. I am filled with dread when we finally set off in convoy—he will lead me to the nearest entrance to the motor-way, called the péage, then I am truly on my own for the first time.

8

THE CAR IS CERTAINLY nippy, but I am only driving at about 50 mph as I enter the motorway. There are three lanes each way and I am sticking as far to the right as possible, my knuckles white as I grip the steering wheel in terror. Cars and trucks flash past me at what seems like 150 mph and the small car shudders with the vibrations as they pass. Then it starts raining—I haven't a clue where to find the windscreen wipers and I'm too frightened to take my eyes off the road. I fumble wildly with various controls and eventually the wipers start up. Gradually I increase my speed and my heartbeat slows marginally. I keep telling myself, over and over, that in a week or so I will be laughing at this. That I will be driving with complete confidence and wondering how I could ever have been so frightened.

As various road signs start appearing along the motorway I realise with apprehension that I haven't the vaguest clue what they mean. How could I be so arrogant as to start driving in a foreign country without any knowledge of the local road rules or without any understanding of the traffic signs and signals? It's lunacy. I feel completely overwhelmed by my own stupidity. At least I have had the commonsense to write out a list of towns and turnoffs which I must take to get to Arles in the Camargue region, my first overnight stay. I have decided to take three days getting to the southwest, firstly to 'enjoy' the drive and see some countryside, secondly to avoid getting stressed by driving too far on any one day. If only I had known that the sheer act of driving itself would have me in such a state.

I stop for lunch at Aix-en-Provence but find negotiating my way in and out of the town and back onto the motorway quite alarming. By late afternoon I see the sign for Arles and cheer myself on. After driving in and out of the town four times, finally, a good hour later, I see the sign to the hotel where David and I have stayed before—The Hotel Gauguin—a comfortable two-star with tall windows and shutters that open onto a gorgeous square. I park in a narrow space with great difficulty, book in and leave in search of a bar. In the shadow of the 2,000-year-old Roman amphitheatre, I find a place where I quickly knock back two huge beers—twice the size of a traditional pint—to the amazement of the proprietor. I feel I need a large hit of alcohol to steady my nerves after the harrowing drive, and it's a reward for having survived my first day alone. So great is the quantity of fluid in my bladder that I need to pee three times before I am fit to wander the back streets and squares in the balmy twilight. Arles is a beautiful city—David and I loved being here eight years ago. There is evidence everywhere of Roman occupation. Apart from the amphitheatre where bullfights are still held regularly in the summer, there is a magnificent Roman theatre which stands by a shady park in the centre of town; there are Roman baths and Cryptoportiques, dark and gloomy underground corridors that were excavated for reasons still not clear to archaeologists. Arles is where Vincent Van Gogh lived for two years, frenetically producing more than two hundred paintings during this short period; indeed this was the place where he finally lost the plot and sliced off his ear, to the dismay of the locals who petitioned for him to be institutionalised. Fellow artist Gauguin lived with Van Gogh during part of this period, which is why so many streets and buildings bear his name—including the hotel where I am staying. Being close to Spain, the city has a distinctive Latin atmosphere. In the square where most of the restaurants are located, flamenco guitarists and dancers wander between tables, busking for francs as diners quaff litres of local wine. It's sheer bliss for an exhausted Australian woman.

Back at the hotel I realise that I have been given the same room that I shared with David on our previous visit. Like many old hotels, the rooms have been bastardised by the inclusion of a small bathroom in one corner to cater for foreign tourists' desire for an 'en suite'. The aperture to the shower recess is so narrow that David became firmly wedged getting in, and I had to free him by liberally applying soap to his belly, after I managed to stop laughing. But only now do I realise just how ridiculously small the bathroom is, typical however of so many two- and three-star French pensions. I sleep very soundly but wake with some dread of the day ahead.

It's funny how in long-term relationships the partners take on different roles and stick to them. David has a naturally good sense of direction and is always confident when driving in foreign countries so I have always left this onerous aspect of our travel to him. I have never been good at map reading and navigating, so he has always plotted our routes on driving holidays and I have assisted by staying awake and chatting to keep him alert while keeping a constant eye on road signs and directions. I have from time to time done a little of the driving—mainly on motorways—but only after he has planned everything and made it easy for me by getting us up and going in the morning. Now I need to take responsibility for all these issues alone, so I carefully study the map over breakfast and make a list in large writing of all the towns I will need to pass through to reach tonight's destination. I have decided to abandon the motorway and go across country, in the hope of less traffic and that there will be more interesting things to see along the way. I really feel a need to prove to myself that I am limited only by my own fears. Surely I am capable of driving across France alone, given that the maps are easy to read and the sign posting is excellent? My main ally is good concentration—I keep saying over and over to myself, 'Pay attention, pay attention,' because I realise that keeping my wits about me is essential if I am to avoid taking the wrong turn. I love the way the French have erected huge blue arrows to remind drivers in which direction to enter a roundabout: there are roundabouts all over rural France and with so many English tourists swerving all over the roads it would be total chaos if the arrows were not there to jog tired drivers' memories. I know that I would be having to think twice every time I approached a roundabout if that blessed blue arrow wasn't there to reassure me. I later read in an English newspaper that a survey of English travellers to Europe found that sixty per cent of drivers don't understand French road signs and are uncertain about how to approach a roundabout. Knowing that there are lots more drivers like myself negotiating the local roadways certainly doesn't fill my heart with confidence.

Before leaving Arles I dash out to visit the Sunday market and buy some small gifts to take to Jock, who is my only contact in the southwest and who has kindly invited me to stay until I find a place of my own. The Arles market is wealthy and busy and I settle on some spicy sausage, various cheeses, large bunches of garlic and shallots and a jar of regional honey. I also buy myself a colourful woven shopping basket which will be useful during my stay—I loathe using plastic shopping bags.

The trip to Albi is a relative breeze and with every hour behind the wheel my confidence grows. The weather also clears and the countryside is certainly beautiful. I bounce along, feeling chuffed with myself as each town on the handwritten list sitting on the dashboard rolls by. France is a feast for the eyes after the bleak and burdened human landscape of India. In India, except when we travel high in the mountains, it is almost impossible to find a view that is totally appealing—there's always a corner of ugliness or sadness or destruction to spoil the frame. In France it's hard to focus on anything that isn't an absolute delight for the eye to behold: neatly bordered pastures of brilliant green, fat and healthy livestock, stone villages that are charming in every possible way.

When the sign to Albi appears I congratulate myself once again on my sheer brilliance and even though I have a repeat performance of driving in and out of the town for half an hour before I finally find a parking space, I feel for the first time that I am in control of the situation. It feels strange having an ongoing dialogue with myself about the ups and downs of this journey because I am so accustomed to vocalising my every thought to whoever is by my side. Being alone means that I am constantly talking to myself instead—sometimes even out loud—

discussing the details of my surroundings and predicaments.

The cheap hotels in the travel book prove impossible to locate, hiding down incredibly narrow back streets where only experienced drivers would be intrepid enough to venture. Presumably that's why they are cheap—they are totally inaccessible. So with some guilt I book into a relatively expensive hotel which has a prominent car park. I overcome my feelings of guilt pretty quickly because the bathroom is sheer bliss with a huge bathtub where I sit and soak, feeling triumphant. In the warm evening air I wander through this beautiful and ancient city, visiting the imposing Gothic cathedral—the Basilica Cecile— where, since it's Saturday evening, I manage to catch a religious service. The cathedral is reputed to be the largest brick building in the world and there certainly are a lot of bricks to be seen from every angle. It took two centuries to build—from 1282 to 1480—and it looks more like a giant fortress than a place of worship. Inside, however, the frescoes and theatrical organ, which is being played, quite take my breath away. Afterwards I saunter up and down side streets looking for a regional café and eventually discover one that is also way over my budget, but decide what the hell. I order an expensive carafe of rosé and my first cassoulet of the journey. It has been grilled under a flame so that the portions of duck and sausage are deliciously crispy. I couldn't feel happier.

The following morning I allow a couple of hours to explore Albi, thinking that I will no doubt return at some stage during my long stay. Albi is famous as the birthplace of the unhappy Toulouse-Lautrec, and in spite of the fact that after deserting it for Paris he spoke most scathingly of this elegant city, they have put together a fantastic museum in his honour. I find a covered

market which is rather disappointing in its selection of foodstuffs
compared to Arles, but I still manage to pick up some interesting
looking cheeses.

Well fed and rested I set off for Jock's house filled with
renewed confidence, singing 'I am woman, hear me roar' at the
top of my voice because I can't get any reception on the car
radio. Jock has given me quite specific instructions on how to
reach his village from Cahors, where I stop before finishing the
last leg of my journey. Cahors is an ancient town which I
remember driving through a few years ago with David. It will be
my nearest town during the six months I am in the southwest, so
I wander around and take in as much as I can. There are two
large squares in the old part of the town, an imposing cathedral
that took more than four centuries to build, and what must
surely be one of the most beautiful bridges in the world, which
spans the fast-moving Lot River. I decide to eat a light lunch
before descending on Jock, and find a warm-looking café that is
packed with Sunday lunch families. The menu is vast and I opt
for a dish of choucroute, saucisson and pommes. I recognise
sausages and potatoes as part of the dish, but am amazed when
it arrives to discover the choucroute is actually sauerkraut. I am
presented with a vast plate piled high with cabbage, seven or
eight different types of sausage and potatoes, enough for at least
four people. I struggle to get even halfway through the meal.
Knowing I still have a little way to drive I decide against drinking
alcohol, but a large cold beer would have been perfect.

On the last leg from Cahors to St Caprais I don't falter once,
and following the given instructions I take only forty minutes
to reach the village. Jock is waiting out the front with his two,
half-wild black village cats, Shagger and Minnie the Moocher.

I can't believe it—at home I have a fat black female cat, also called Minnie the Moocher. Jock gives me a kiss on each cheek in typical French style and within ten minutes I am sitting at his dining room table clutching a glass of local Cahors red. The adventure has just begun.

9

JOCK'S RETIREMENT RETREAT in the Lot has been affectionately dubbed 'Jock's Trap' by his friends, with a handmade pokerwork sign beside the front door and letters posted from Australia and New York addressed accordingly. It's a simple old stone house in a small fourteenth-century village that time seems to have forgotten. Half the buildings are deserted and there is no shop or café, just an incongruously modern glass phone box and a mailbox that's emptied every day except Sunday. Jock discovered his dream house empty and derelict one summer eight years ago when he was holidaying with his oldest friends, the Barwicks, who have a house nearby and have been coming to the southwest for their summer holidays for more than thirty years. Originally the little house was no more than two rooms and a barn for the animals, but with help from friends and local tradespeople it was lovingly transformed into a comfortable home, with cream walls and pale terracotta-coloured ceramic floor tiles. Jock converted the old barn into a simple kitchen and the vaulted roofline into a second-storey addition, with two bedrooms and a bathroom. Immediately I love the house, and also Jock, who turns out to be one of life's great discoveries.

At first glance Jock's physical appearance is somewhat alarming. He's very tall with a large frame and a handsome thatch of silver grey hair, of which he is rightly proud. His face bears testimony to his passion for red wine and his reluctance to wear a hat during the long, hot summers of southwest France: to say he has a ruddy complexion is an understatement—it's brilliant scarlet. Jock's interests in life do not extend to being even vaguely concerned about his clothes or personal appearance. He's one of those blokes who prefer wellworn, comfortable gear; the only problem is that some of his clothes have been worn to death, with the fabric fraying at the cuffs and falling apart under the slightest stress. And there are many stresses. When Jock bends over it's not unusual to hear the ripping sound of fabric tearing apart. His pants are perilously suspended beneath his rounded belly, held up by a belt that is constantly in need of tightening. In winter, when he can wear a sweatshirt over his usual shirt, he dons braces and this means the trousers are less likely to take a nosedive.

'I was born with no hips,' he laments at least twenty times a day while grappling to catch his strides before they drop to the floor. Sometimes, late in the evening, he isn't quite quick enough.

Jock's many female friends constantly chide him about the way he dresses. He sometimes doesn't get around to shaving for days at a time and he's been known to wear the same daggy clothes until they practically walk around on their own. I wonder to myself if he was dressed like this when he was a medical reporter covering news stories in New York. I suspect so because he proudly tells me how, speaking at his seventieth birthday, our mutual friend Gil referred to him as 'The King of Grunge'. He has a certain style about him. Jock style, like it or lump it. And I like it. Jock and I enjoy all the same things. He adores this part of France and doesn't for one second regret retiring here, in spite of the fact that his grasp of the language is still limited after seven years.

'I keep thinking I've died and gone to heaven,' he exclaims as he proudly shows me around his patch of the woods.

I can't help but agree with him. We spend the first two weeks exploring the mediaeval villages and bastide (or fortified) towns that are the main feature of the Lot. We target villages where there are food markets or antique fairs, planning our evening meals (never less than four courses) and then buying the appropriate ingredients before repairing to a café or restaurant for beer followed by a long lunch. By three every afternoon I am ready to sleep off the food and drink for several hours before rising and starting again—I will need to detox if I keep this up. Jock is exceedingly generous both with his time and his wallet— he routinely insists on shouting me lunch and I regard his personalised insights into French life as a gift. I dub this high-spirited introduction to the region as 'Jock's Tours of the Lot' and can't think of a better way to get established.

Jock and I once worked in the same newspaper building in Sydney in the early 1970s and although I remember his name and reputation clearly from those days, I feel certain that he barely remembers me. At that time I was a young reporter, just out of my cadetship and working on a trashy television magazine while he was a top-ranking showbusiness columnist. We often rubbed shoulders at film premieres and television program launches, but never really mixed socially. Bumping along the leafy lanes on our sightseeing tours we reminisce nonstop and quickly discover a great many friends and colleagues in common. His anecdotes about his life and work are endless and hilarious, and I identify strongly with his attitude to life. Born in New Zealand in the wealthy country township of Wanganui, he started his career as a young newspaperman in the 1950s, then travelled to Sydney where he worked on various daily papers first as a reporter and sub editor, later as a showbusiness writer and columnist. The last sixteen years of his working life were in New York, where he was a columnist on a mass-circulation Murdoch magazine. He covered a wide range of topics, including health and medicine, and as a result is quite witty and knowledgeable on a vast array of subjects, from stomach ulcers to arthouse films. He loves good jazz music and poetry and antiquated television— I am forever catching him watching old reruns of ''Allo, 'Allo' and 'Dr Who' on his satellite television.

When Jock shouts me lunch and I make noises of protest he invariably says, 'But I've got money I haven't even spent yet.' He sometimes suggests it can be my turn next time round, and we'll go somewhere much more expensive. When I agree without hesitation to his proposal of a drink at the local bar or a meal at a nearby restaurant he declares, 'You're easier to get than a packet of Rothmans.' Jock is generous to a fault and kind-hearted—nothing ever seems to be too much trouble. He never fails to surprise and amuse at dinner parties. I've seen a pair of conservative ladies blanch when he suddenly bursts into verse:

'Hooray, hooray, it's the first of May,
Outdoor fucking starts today.'

Jock has developed an extensive network of English-speaking friends who are never surprised to see him turn up with a visitor in tow because his house has, quite understandably, become a regular holiday destination for a raft of ragged overseas colleagues—both men and women—who enjoy his unending hospitality, warmth and wit. We scoot around the country lanes together, dropping in unannounced here and there for an aperitif, filling our days and evenings with nonstop eating, drinking and sightseeing. I keep saying to myself that I must start taking walks or getting some form of exercise, but it's very hot and sitting in the cool of Jock's house with its tiled floors and thick walls sipping a chilled rosé seems like a much better idea. Already my pants are getting hard to zip up, not a good beginning when I have firmly imagined that this long, relaxing break from work will have me returning home looking slim, tanned and thoroughly well rested.

Not long after arriving my fiftieth birthday looms. It feels odd being so far away from home for such a landmark occasion, but I am determined to enjoy it regardless. Jock's in the know, having been emailed by Gil, and we discover that there is to be a special lunch in the restaurant across the road from his cottage, so it couldn't be more perfect. We can eat and drink as much as we like, without having to drive anywhere afterwards.

The morning of my birthday is cold and overcast. I spend more than half an hour talking to my family in Australia who are having a typical Sunday roast dinner to celebrate my birthday as well as David's, which falls two days before. The previous day was the winter solstice in Australia and the annual Winter Magic Festival in Katoomba has apparently been a great success, with our grandchildren donning fancy dress for a street parade and an evening of fun at the local pub which has left some members of the family feeling a little hungover. Hence the lateness of the midday birthday meal. I speak to everyone properly for the first time since I left home, except for Eamonn who is still refusing to talk about me or acknowledge me on the phone. David says he's just being a typical sulky six-year-old, but I recognise his feelings of abandonment, and that his silence is a form of punishment. He'll get over it I'm sure, but I find it a bit painful knowing he feels so miffed.

Jock is preparing a caviar mousse and we have put champagne on ice for the drinks party to be held after the lunch, with a group of seven of Jock's wayward friends along for the ride. The restaurant across the road doesn't operate on a regular basis, however in order to maintain a current liquor licence it is legally obliged to open at least four times a year. The solution is a series of monthly Sunday lunches, with the set menu being distributed by pamphlet ten days ahead of time. Jock's assorted friends arrive at midday for a drink. They are a funny lot—two elderly retired English couples living nearby, an English man of middle years restoring an old house, and a raging Scottish couple who are down for a month to work on their barn. The meal, which is typical of the region, starts with huge steaming bowls of garlicky chicken soup and noodles with chunks of country-style bread. The charcuterie course is overwhelming, with several choices of pâté and terrine plus crudités based on tomato and raw carrot. The poulet plat du jour, chicken served with verjuice and creamy potatoes, is followed by a crisp salad, then an elaborate cheese board and an even more elaborate dessert, a fruity flan with lashings of cream. The wine never stops flowing and the local liquor is passed around with our coffee. Called 'eau de vie' it's made from pears or plums and it's nothing more than firewater, but somehow as it sears down my throat, it rounds off the three-and-a-half hour epic eat-a-thon.

Weaving out into the afternoon air we return to Jock's court-yard for the champagne and caviar party. I feel quite delightfully unsober, but several in the group are really starting to look much more the worse for wear, lurching and slurring. More of Jock's friends arrive bearing gifts, which is quite a surprise given that I have known them less than two weeks. But somehow they have already tuned into my Australian sense of humour, and the gifts reflect this: an Aussie bush hat with swinging tampons instead of corks; a vulgar barbecue apron with false plastic breasts, featuring unseemly slogans in French. It's good to see a strong thread of bad taste running through French culture. I sleep soundly after my birthday party and wonder the following morning what form the celebration would have taken had I stayed at home. Most probably it would have been a Sunday lunch for the immediate family of fifteen which I would have planned, shopped for and cooked, with David clearing up and doing the dishes.

One thing I puzzle over while I am staying at Jock's is the way in which I position myself to sleep now that I am alone in a bed. Instead of spreading myself out and luxuriating in the space that's suddenly available, I curl up on my usual side and never venture onto the other side of the bed at all. The sheets and pillowcases on David's side of the bed remain smooth and untouched. I assume it's just a force of habit, after so many years of accommodating his shape alongside me. But I wish I could thrash about and make use of the entire bed space, rather than keeping so tidily to one side.

10

EVEN QUITE WELL-TRAVELLED friends, who are familiar with Provence, the Dordogne, Normandy and the Loire valley, are rarely aware of the department known as the Lot. Indeed, before I arrived, I had seen it on the map and largely dismissed it as a rural no-man's land; which it is, in the sense that it lacks overdevelopment and industrialisation. But what it lacks in modernity and sophistication it makes up for tenfold in old-world charm and grace.

This is one of the oldest parts of France, rich in history and steeped in a cultural and agricultural tradition that is still very much in evidence to this day. It's a hidden treasure, although now that the Dordogne has become over-popular with tourists, and with foreigners buying second homes, eyes are turning to this tranquil place. The department takes its name from the free-flowing Lot River, which winds through vineyards and townships and is crossed at various points by wonderfully romantic ancient stone bridges.

Tranquil is exactly the right word for the Lot, because this area is the least populated in all of Europe, with a current head count not very different from that of Roman times. It was not always so, because during various phases of its history, the Lot boasted thriving towns and villages and a very rich economy. Now, however, it has suffered the fate of rural areas all over the world—an exodus of the young population who, once educated, seek larger towns and cities and a more modern lifestyle. It is their loss.

The way in which France is divided into various territories can be very confusing, because it hasn't been neatly portioned into states with well-defined borders, and there are layers of names, some dating back to Roman times, which are still in use in conjunction with modern names. The southwest of France, for example, is also known by the ancient name of Aquitaine, but in many maps, weather charts and newspapers it is also called Suds Ouest. Within the southwest are several departments including the Lot, which also carries the ancient name of Quercy.

Likewise the department of the Dordogne is also still frequently referred to as Périgord, its name from ancient times. The region has been peopled since prehistoric times and archaeological evidence shows that the warm valleys dotted with caves must have been the most favourable environment for the evolution of human species in all of Europe. There are well over one hundred decorated caves dated between 30000 and 10000 BC in southwest France, some of which are open to the public during the summer season. Visiting them, you get a spine-tingling feeling realising how long people have walked on this part of the earth, almost as long as the Aboriginal people are thought to have inhabited Australia. Modern farmers still turn up flints and other prehistoric tools when they plough their fields—they rise to the surface if it rains immediately after ploughing—and it's not uncommon to see a small collection of museum pieces decorating a shelf or coffee table.

In the past the landscape here has been called harsh and even savage, possibly because of the wild and arid limestone plateaux known as causses. Here the natural vegetation is scarce and windswept, but although the soil is said to be poor I don't find the fields and vineyards reflecting a lack of richness. All around I see scrub oak and junipers, fields of corn, hillsides dotted with healthy-looking sheep and cattle. There are duck and geese farms in evidence outside most villages, and brilliant hopper bins of bright orange corncobs for fattening the animals for market.

During the sixth to fourth centuries BC, when it was known as Gaul, many regions of France were invaded by Celtic tribes. Cahors remains the largest town in the Lot and early records show that it was originally a settlement during these pre-Roman times, named after the Gaulish tribe Cadurcii. When I stop to wonder why I feel so at home in this foreign place, I consider this Celtic link. As a pure Celt of Irish, Welsh and Scottish extraction, I feel that my genes may somehow be shared with the descendants of the ancient tribespeople who ran like savages across this land when it was barely touched by human habitation. They were small and dark like the people of Wales, and the people here in the Lot look similar to them to this very day, with Roman blood mixed in of course. Maybe my connection to this place goes back far further than my connection to Australia. Or so I fantasise. With my red hair and pale, freckled complexion, however, I certainly look nothing like a local.

The period of history that is most fascinating is the twelfth century, when Eleanor of Aquitaine presided over her French and English kingdoms from here, constantly travelling with her vast entourage in and around Quercy on her journeys. I manage to get hold of a recently published biography of Eleanor, just released in the UK, and pore over the details of this amazing woman's life. So many places that I am familiar with are mentioned in the book, including Cahors which was seized for Eleanor by her husband, the English King Henry, in 1159; Rocamadour, where she made a pilgrimage bearing rich gifts in the middle of the century; and nearby Puy-l'Evêque where in 1138, while still married to the French King Louis, she attended a religious festival. It almost makes me shiver to imagine how this place must have looked during her reign; this sense of continuity, this seamless link with history, appeals to my imagination so much. You could easily shoot a film about Eleanor in any one of a number of old towns and villages in this region, and they would appear very much as they did when she was alive. Just take down a few power poles and remove the odd satellite dish and you could be right there by her side. I often experience a strong feeling of this when I am exploring nearby towns and villages, especially midweek when the streets are so often bare of people and there are few cars around to ruin the mediaeval images I love to conjure in my mind's eye.

Even older are the Neolithic remains of human dwellings and religious sites that can be found in and around ordinary towns like Prayssac. Jock and I are taken on a guided tour of these by a lively American couple who make a living writing outrageously witty travel guides. Dana and Michael, who have made their home here, have studied the entire southwest of France in detail, and their knowledge of its history is undoubtedly more extensive than many of the locals, whose families have been living here for generations. Following their car, we drive past a bland modern housing development on the outskirts of Prayssac to reach an amazing circuit of ancient structures known as dolmens, which resemble small versions of Stonehenge with massive platform rocks suspended on hefty uprights. In the same area is a circle of menhirs—huge rocks that have been thrust into the ground as upright pillars, also known to have had strong religious significance for the ancient people who lived here. There's a rock-carved niche, known as 'Caesar's Armchair', and a most unusual gariotte, or stone shepherd's hut, with two chambers instead of the usual single shelter. We are astounded to think of these treasures just sitting here in the woodlands, unprotected and largely ignored. The fact that so few people seem to know about the dolmens and menhirs probably helps to preserve them, but I wonder if the people living in the rather plain modern houses just down the hillside are aware that their tract of land has such a rich and mysterious history.

As my interests lie so much in the survival skills and daily lifestyle of ordinary people, I am attracted to a guided tour of farms that is advertised at one of the tourism offices. Again I drag Jock along for the ride, which involves driving our own car and following a bilingual guide through the winding country lanes around Belvès, a hillside township about half an hour from St Caprais. The tour includes lunch at a ferme auberge, or farm restaurant, which serves food that is actually produced right there on the farm. Our tour begins with a detailed look at a tobacco farm; the tobacco industry was once the mainstay of the region but is now falling from favour because of the changing tastes of smokers. The dark-leafed heavy tobacco variety grown successfully for decades is now no longer desired because smokers prefer the lighter and paler leaf varieties that simply don't do as well in the local soils and climates. As the farmer points out, growing tobacco is a tremendously labour intensive task, and one which also uses a lot of chemicals because the crops require frequent spraying against pests and diseases during the main growing season. Driving around the southwest, I often see empty tobacco-drying sheds—they are always taller than the local barns with timber-slatted sides that are opened, like louvres, to allow gentle breezes through while the crops are hanging to dry. Fields that were once used to grow tobacco have now been turned over to maize or wheat as farmers try to keep up with the changing pace of agriculture. In the morning we also briefly visit a goat cheese farm, where the friendly goats crowd around us and try eating our loose clothing and camera bag straps. The smell of goat urine is quite distinctive, and I always think it carries over into the cheese, which is why I prefer the more subtle flavour of sheep cheese.

Our lunch at the local ferme auberge is an eye-opener. All eight of us are invited into the family dining room after being given a brief tour of the farm and its buildings. I am totally besotted with the old but reliable bread oven in the barn, built of stone with a rounded back and chimney; it once baked crusty loaves for the entire hamlet, and now bakes fresh bread for the restaurant at least three times a week. Just about everything that passes our lips has been made on the farm. There's a strongly alcoholic aperitif made from plums, chicken soup with noodles and, of course, great chunks of fresh cooked bread. There are crudités from the garden and large portions of roasted duck—from the same family we have just seen shuffling around the poultry pen. The red wine is also made on the spot, and is quite light and aromatic compared with some of the heavier Cahors-style wines. After the required five courses we are back on track to visit a goose and duck farm where the most famous delicacy is produced: foie gras. I am not actually looking forward to this part of the tour, having heard so many grim stories about the suffering of the poor birds. However the agony is minimised with just a short demonstration of force feeding— I feel certain that when it's done to a mass of birds the effects would be more distressing. The victim goose on show is quite cheerful as the tube is inserted into his gullet, but is incapable of getting back onto his webbed feet after the dose of corn has been pumped down his throat.

We are then taken through the whole production line, and fortunately there's no slaughtering during our visit. Still the smell of blood remains in the air, and when at the end of the tour we are offered a tray of foie gras, I can't participate, especially after having stuffed my face so heartily at lunchtime. The others, however, do not share my queasiness and tuck in as though they haven't eaten for a week.

I am constantly impressed by how uncomplicated the lives of the rural people seem to be. In many ways they are without the unnecessary trappings that we regard as essential. Their lives follow the seasons and the harvests and as a result their needs are very straightforward compared to those of people who live in the city. Even though they now have all the modern conveniences of electricity, phones, computers and email, a modern pace does not seem to impinge too much on the ritual of their daily lives. Lunch is probably the most important thing in their daily agenda. I can't help but admire this attitude.

11

JOCK'S SMALL VILLAGE IS typical of hundreds. Those buildings of St Caprais not empty and derelict are occupied mostly by farmers, both active and retired. The church, with its Romanesque apse raised in the fourteenth century, is externally austere yet reveals some faint but fascinating murals on the interior walls. There was gossip for some years that the murals would qualify the church to be classified as an historic monument, but they turned out to be not quite as old as the villagers had hoped. They are greatly treasured, regardless. There are drystone tiles, called lauzes, in the apse, also dating back more than seven hundred years. The bell is still rung twice a day—to call the farm workers in for lunch at 12.15 and again at sundown for dinner, which is well after 9 pm in the summer and as early as 4.45 pm in deepest winter. The ringing of the bell is the self-imposed undertaking of the village's most prominent farming wife, Madame Dalmas, whose husband Claude is a direct descendant of one of the oldest families in the area. The Dalmas family has been ringing the bell ever since the full-time priest left, more than fifteen years ago.

Looking closely at her face, I estimate that Mme Dalmas is no more than a few years older than I am. She is small, dark-haired and dynamic. I try to compare our lives as women of a similar vintage, but it's quite impossible. She has barely moved from her home since birth, and while she and I have both reared children while working simultaneously, there the comparison ends abruptly. Her entire life has revolved around the farm and her family. She tends a large vegetable garden which supplies them all year round and is so productive that armfuls of leafy greens, tomatoes and pumpkin are given away to friends and neighbours—Jock is certainly a beneficiary of this largess. Mme Dalmas also keeps a large flock of hens for eggs and meat, and rears ducks and geese each summer for making confit and other poultry-related delicacies. She is responsible for a flock of sheep which she moves from meadow to meadow almost every day. She has a small dog to assist her, and as there are no fences except for the main holding field, she has to watch them for literally hours every day, seated on a cushion, reading a magazine. I often see her keeping an eye on her charges from under a tree in the late afternoon dappled light. The sheep follow her voice quite obediently, though the dog doesn't appear nearly as well trained.

Mme Dalmas cooks two large, hot meals a day in the French tradition for her family—a son who works the farm with his father and the daughters still living at home. There are soups, terrines, pâtés and stews, and always a dessert. She doesn't drive and seldom leaves the village to shop; her bread is delivered and a grocery truck comes calling every Wednesday morning with the basic necessities—cleaning products, butter, sugar and flour. A butcher's van also delivers various cuts of meat that the farm itself does not provide. I never see her at the weekly markets in Prayssac or Cazals—she would be far too busy to take time off for marketing. She works from dawn to dusk, and I never see her without a smile on her face and a warm greeting. There are only about twenty people living in St Caprais, and many of them are quite elderly and live alone. Mme Dalmas takes food from her pantry to many of them. She is a vital link between the different village families.

There are several ruined buildings around the village, with doors and shutters that have fallen away with time, although there is also a large old building that has recently been quite beautifully restored. There are some handsome houses only occupied in the summer by holidaymakers, and a holiday let, known as a gite, that is rented out to Dutch and Germans on a regular basis. The restaurant across the road, the one where I celebrated my birthday, is the only focal point attracting out-siders into the village on a regular basis. The streets are narrow but are used constantly by farming vehicles moving from one field to the next. During the height of summer when the wheat and maize are ready to cut, a combine harvester somehow squeezes around the main corner—Jock is asked to move his car from the front of his house so that it can rumble past. I am constantly amazed at how these massive tractors and earth-moving machines negotiate the narrow streets designed for simple carts.

Just outside the village is a moss-covered washing place that links into the stream, where women once came daily to launder their clothes and linen. In the village itself are two small squares where community meals and celebrations are held at various times of the year. Outside the door of every occupied dwelling are overflowing pots and tubs of geraniums, petunias and begonias that stand out so wonderfully against the warm, buttery stonework. Not far from Jock's house is a neatly tended old cemetery with high drystone walls and quite elaborate family crypts. In a levelled sandy area near the cemetery boules is sometimes played by those villagers who have the time in their busy farming schedules. Occasionally we newcomers indulge in a game amongst ourselves, playing more noisily and with far less skill than the locals.

As I drive or walk around the countryside that surrounds St Caprais the odd modern building or house not quite in keeping with the old style appears from time to time. Otherwise the scene is consistently one of mediaeval villages or perfectly groomed fields of maize or wheat. The livestock gleam with glossy coats and bulging bellies, unlike the pathetic emaciated and worm-riddled herds I saw on the trip in India. The countryside, when I first start exploring in late spring, is more perfect than a picture postcard could ever depict. After early rains the crops are galloping ahead and after a week of hot and sunny weather, the hay has been quickly harvested and rolled into giant 'boules' around the fields for gathering and storing at a later date. The hay can't be stacked in barns for several months as the heat generated within each boule is dynamite and can easily self combust; they must be left out until they start to break down before being stored for the winter months.

All around the landscape are stone walls, and almost every one has a rose growing against it, mostly deep vermilion or scarlet: it is the perfect colour against the bright light and piercing blue sky. The odd white or pale pink rose seems wishy washy and out of place by comparison.

St Caprais is set at the conjunction of several small hills, giving it views to the surrounding farmland. This was planned initially so that all approaches to the little town would be visible, to give the villagers time to rush inside the fortified church should strangers or enemies approach from any direction. The church has no windows and sombre metre-thick walls just for this purpose. The aspect also means that as I walk or drive towards St Caprais from any perspective I see the church prominently towering above the domestic dwellings. So often the churches are by far the most imposing structures in a small settlement. There is one corner approaching St Caprais that leads from the washing place up past several neatly farmed meadows, and every time I drive or walk it, no matter what time of day, my heart simply soars with pleasure as I round the corner and the village suddenly comes into view.

I have to admit that moments of sheer, unadulterated delight such as this are few and far between in my 'real' life. I certainly love driving out through the Australian countryside and have a deep love and appreciation of both the bush and the cleared farmland. But I seldom feel such a lurch of happiness at a view or vista as I am experiencing here in France. Perhaps it's just an unaccustomed sense of exhilaration, having cast off my responsibilities and allowed my emotions finally to run free.

12

BEFORE THE 1960S THERE were very few foreigners
living in southwest France, however with the decline
of the population and the gradual awareness in
the outside world of its superior weather and cheap property
prices, the situation has dramatically changed. Old deserted
chateaux and farmhouses have been snapped up as holiday
homes by English and Dutch families, eager to spend part of
each summer in rural retreat. The farming families generally
found adjusting to their foreign neighbours difficult at first,
but were soon delighted to see derelict buildings being restored
to their former glory, and quickly came to appreciate the
economic benefits of a slightly expanded population, even if
they were English. Tradespeople have benefited by getting work
restoring roofs and chipping render from ancient stonework
for newcomers who prefer the look of exposed stone rather
than grey concrete render. Plumbers, tilers, electricians and
glaziers are suddenly in demand, and the local cafés, restaurants
and alimentations (general stores) have also enjoyed a revival.

In my dreaming and fantasising about living in France—long before setting off on this adventure—I visualised myself mixing with very few English-speaking people. I imagined days, even weeks, passing without a single conversation in my own language, and anticipated having constant contact with French speakers that would vastly improve my language skills. I expected to spend many hours sitting alone in cafés; I would also spend long, quiet evenings reading, writing and sewing, and enjoy vast stretches of solitude. This was going to be my thinking time.

Nothing could be further from my life now in St Caprais. Within hours of parking my car outside Jock's Trap I was sipping red wine with a handful of his English-speaking expatriate friends, and now as the days and weeks roll by the numbers of new people I meet multiplies dramatically. There are New Zealanders and a scattering of Americans, Canadians, South Africans and Australians who have chosen to spend either their retirement or a part of every summer in the Lot. I find the mix of English speakers as diverse in character and personality as in any blended community, with the usual sprinkling of eccentrics and misfits who are invariably more comfortable when away from their native habitats. A lot of the English who have chosen to settle permanently in this part of France have not spent the vast majority of their working lives in the UK, and have therefore found it difficult to adjust to the reality of settling back in their homeland on a full-time basis. The appalling English weather gets to them, as does the way the 'old country' has changed so dramatically these last few decades. Those I meet who are just on holiday for a month or two seem to be in permanent party mode, hosting lunches, dinners and drinks parties to make the most of the abundant food and wine, not to mention the gorgeous weather. So this is why, within a week of arriving, I find myself in a nonstop rush of social engagements, lurching from one laden table to another, from drinks parties to four-hour lunches to suppers where we don't even sit down to eat until well after 10 pm. All of this requires a tremendous amount of stamina because it involves quaffing copious quantities of wine and beer. Over three weeks I realise I haven't had one night 'in' before midnight, and my waistline is rapidly starting to exceed the limits of even my most capacious jeans.

Jock's oldest friends are the Barwicks. These are the people he visited every summer from New York until he 'got the bug' and bought a French cottage of his own. David and Margaret Barwick fled New Zealand in the 1950s and initially lived in the UK where David, a lawyer, joined the British Colonial Service (later renamed the more politically correct Department of Overseas Development), and took his family to various far-flung postings. Over a period of forty years they have lived and worked in outposts including Africa, the British Virgin Islands (where David was the Governor) and the Caymans (where he was Attorney General). On retirement the Barwicks originally planned to spend half the year in the Caymans and half in France, but have ended up as full-time residents of the Lot, living in a sympathetically restored farmhouse and barn. They have one of the best gardens around—indeed to my delight I learn that Margaret is a semi-retired garden designer. During her long career, apart from planning and establishing two botanical gardens in the tropics where they were posted, she spent several years recently writing the definitive book on tropical trees. Their garden is very untypical of rural France. It has deep beds and borders spilling over with glorious roses, fragrant perennials, and gaily flowering annuals crammed into every nook and cranny. There are sweeping lawns and climbing roses and clematis that have been allowed to shoot up into trees and over archways in flowering profusion. Margaret and David are also both keen artists and the garden reflects their understanding of colour and texture in planting combinations. There are splashes of brilliant scarlet among beds of yellows and oranges, and areas where the cooler purples and blues predominate. Margaret constantly runs the garden down, saying it is totally unplanned and full of clashing colours, but to my eye it is a gem hidden behind high walls and wrought iron gates. By contrast, the farmers' gardens are just trees and lawn with the odd climbing rose and potted geranium, so finding a complex English country-style garden is quite a thrill.

Like most people who retire to the Lot the Barwicks love to eat and drink and socialise and are therefore, in my view, very easy people to fall in with. They certainly work hard in the garden during the day, but love to ease off in the late afternoon for casual drinks or dinners at a colourful table set out on the lawn just near the kitchen door. In their retirement they have also become dedicated vegetable gardeners, with a large potager in the French style that is overburdened with produce at the height of the season. We feast regularly from their garden, harvesting tomatoes and lettuce, beans, beetroot, sweet corn, carrots, eggplants and capsicums. It's almost TOO much—in fact they tell me that the family motto is 'Only Too Much is Enough', which suits my hedonistic holiday tendencies. Their farmhouse is called Les Mespoules and it is nestled in a hamlet of farms just a short walk from St Caprais. Any time I drop by, except perhaps first thing in the morning, the bar is open.

The Barwicks' older daughter Jan also lives in the region. She is blonde, beautiful and married to a landscape gardener called Philippe, who is one of the few people I can struggle to practise my very bad French on. Philippe has a thriving business looking after the gardens of both locals and part-time holiday residents and he has a wonderful way of working with the rough-hewn stone, constructing impressive drystone walls and even recreating a broken down shepherd's hut, which has become a major feature in one of his client's gardens. Philippe experiences totally different gardening problems to those I am accustomed to dealing with in Australia, and I love listening to him talk about his daily landscaping trials and tribulations. Moles are a major nuisance, especially on formal lawns or areas that have been smoothed over for croquet or boules. The nurseries sell a repellent with a cute picture of a mole on the package, that is inserted into mole hills and apparently makes them want to leave town in a big hurry; Philippe also uses some vicious-looking traps that fire a metal bullet into the mole's skull as it burrows gaily along, unaware of impending disaster. Deer that nibble and ringbark young trees are also a problem, and many new plantings require elaborate tree guards during the first few years of their life. The deer adore the sweet young bark, and can destroy an entire garden planting in just a few hours. Many of the gardens are open, without any form of fencing, and there is always the risk of cattle getting in, or worse still, wild boars, which can turn a manicured lawn upside-down in a matter of minutes. Because a lack of water has never been a critical problem, mulching hasn't really caught on yet in French gardening, so I enjoy giving Philippe some background information about all the mulching methods that we use so extensively in Australian gardens. Within a few weeks of my arrival he starts experimenting with mulch, and certainly finds it boosts plant growth and helps to keep the weeds down.

Philippe is often helped with his landscaping work by Jan who has come to love gardening and, being a clever, artistic type, has developed a great natural skill for putting plants together sympathetically in beds and borders. Her use of colour in both flowers and foliage adds greatly to the charm of many local gardens which Philippe constructs and maintains, mostly for expatriats who prefer English-style landscapes with their deep flower beds and borders. I find Jan and Philippe to be great fun, and we spend a lot of time together exploring some of the local tourist attractions and joining in village feasts and celebrations.

One afternoon, while Jan's younger sister Miranda and brother-in-law Tim are visiting from America, we set out to explore the amazing underground river system known as Gouffre de Padirac, which is located over the border into the Dordogne. Gouffre, which means 'hole', refers to the incredible gaping entrance to this maze of river caves which is thirty metres in diameter. In ancient times the darkly mysterious hole, which is nearly one hundred metres deep and seems to have been created by some huge volcanic explosion, was believed to be the entrance to hell. This explains why it wasn't explored and revealed to the public until relatively recently—the late nineteenth century, in fact.

We descend by lift and stairs to the base of the chasm, and despite the fact that it's nearly forty degrees outside, once in the caves we need to rug up with warm jackets—inside, it's a constant thirteen degrees all year round. Romantic shallow timber boats, manned by gondoliers dressed in period costume, take us winding through a section of the caves, giving a humorous commentary which Jan cheerfully translates for our benefit. There are more than twenty-two miles of caves in the system, but the ninety-minute tour takes us to just a few of them. The lighting that has been set up to highlight the most dramatic and cavernous limestone formations is very dated, with ugly wires strung from one glaring bulb to another; it was obviously established many decades ago and has never been improved. I wonder how it must have been for those early explorers brave enough to enter the depths of this river system, seeing it all for the first time by candlelight. It's a most extraordinary place, and very popular with tourists in the height of the season. We are fortunate to have visited before the school holidays, when apparently it's not uncommon to queue for several hours just to get in. The boatmen are the sons and grandsons of the first boatmen to take tourists through the cool depths of the Padirac river system, and the rights to man the boats (and collect the huge tips) are passed along from father to son; it's a highly prized profession. Our boatman seems to think it's amusing to rock the small vessel violently while we are negotiating some narrow but deep passageways, which doesn't please Miranda, who finds the entire experience quite claustrophobic. We are more than happy to find our feet back firmly on rock, and clamber quickly up to the brilliant light and warmth of the summer afternoon.

I find it refreshing to come in contact with people who know absolutely nothing about me or my background. The people of Jock's social set have no idea where I fit into the world. They have no concept of my parents, my husband, my children, my home or my work. We so often categorise people according to the trappings of their life, making judgments based on preconceived notions of where they fit into the social scheme of things. Here I am simply an anonymous woman from the other side of the world. Unattached, without any baggage, I have no status. In a sense it is like being a teenager from a small country town who longs to escape to the big city where nobody knows who they are. No nosy neighbours or friends of the family to report back on any misdeeds or misadventures. It's such a novel sensation being an unknown quantity after five decades of being my father's daughter in the world of journalism; my husband's wife in the film industry; my children's mother in the local school community; the gardener's friend in the world of television lifestyle shows. Here I am just me. It's wonderful.

I also quickly realise that I am now socialising more than I have for decades, and that back in my 'real' life, friendships and entertaining have been abandoned for other priorities, such as my increasingly busy career and ever-expanding family. I have dozens of friends at home who I see only once or twice a year— perhaps communicating more by phone or email—but rarely sitting around a table and sharing a meal. Suddenly I am surrounded by a small but solid group of interesting individuals with whom I seem to have formed an instant bond. We are in constant communication, planning meals together or outings to all the summer activities in the surrounding villages and towns. So instead of being alone, sewing and reading and gazing at my navel, I am in the thick of an intense social whirl. And I am determined to make more time for friendships when I return home.

13

AFTER SEVERAL WEEKS OF camping at Jock's I am no closer to finding a place of my own to live. There is a promise of a house for three months from September, but that's two-and-a-half months away. There are dozens of houses around that are used for only four or six weeks a year; they are mainly owned by English families or people from Paris who holiday during the height of the season and then leave the house deserted for the rest of the year. Jock thinks that one particular couple might be happy for their summer house to be occupied rather than empty, and might even allow me to stay rent free in return for tending the garden and mowing the extensive lawns, however it's not yet available and I really need to find alternative accommodation in the meantime. Rentals are at their peak because it's the 'high' season and most available places have been tarted up for family holidays and are either too large or too expensive for me. Jock meanwhile keeps saying that I can stay as long as I like.

'I'm in no hurry to throw her out,' he tells friends who

enquire about my house-hunting prospects.

I appreciate how comfortable it must be for Jock having a warm body around—and a built-in drinking and eating mate—but I feel anxious to find my own space where I can begin my experiment in living alone. After all, that is the main purpose of my escape. Jock has run out of ideas and there are few new leads. Lying in bed at night I even start feeling a little desperate. If I cannot become more proactive I'll still be in Jock's Trap in six weeks or eight weeks or even six months' time. It will be fun but I'll not be experiencing what I set out to achieve.

When I finally find some cheap alternative accommodation, it's more by good luck than by good management. Lunching at the restaurant across the road one Sunday, I ask one of the fluent French speakers at our table to make some enquiries with the restaurant owners, Jean and Lisette, who I've been told own property and have business interests all around the district. To my delight I learn they have a small studio apartment suitable for a single person on the ground level behind their shop in Ville-franche-du-Périgord, a fourteenth-century fortified town just across the border into the Dordogne. Lisette has offered to drive me the following day, for an inspection. The best news, from my point of view, is that the rent is only 1200 ff per month—about $75 a week, or $11 a night—including electricity. It is furnished and equipped with kitchen appliances, Lisette says, but I will need to provide my own linen.

I have been to the small town of Villefranche several times with Jock and love its open square, covered market and narrow main street of unpretentious shops. Unlike a lot of the ancient fortified or bastide towns it manages to sustain a couple of good hotel bars, a restaurant and pizzeria without being overtly touristy.

There are also a couple of first-rate boulangeries and char-
cuteries. The street Lisette takes me to is Rue Saint George,
parallel to the main street on the low side, and equally as narrow
although sealed with asphalt, not cobbled. The buildings, many
very old and graceful with shuttered windows and stone towers,
back onto this street, which is consequently faced with a myriad
of small windows and access doors or garages that once would
have been barns. My room is on the ground floor of a handsome
three-storey, narrow building and it has two tall timber-shuttered
windows—very old, very French. The main door is always
unlocked, and the door to the 'studio' as it is euphemistically
called, is just inside to the left. It was obviously quite a grand
house which has been divided up into small flats or gites for
renting to tourists in the summer. The floors of the studio are
polished timber, and the walls are sponged in a soft yellow that is
not unlike my bedroom at home. I find the atmosphere instantly
charming, but it's the fine detail that really captures my imagination. The kitchen, which is about 1.5 metres square, is tucked
under a curved staircase with barely enough headroom for
anyone of average height to stand upright in front of the stove.
When I start cooking, if I stand on my toes, my head will bang into
the underneath of the stairs. The bed is a double, quite clean
and comfortable, and hidden behind a garish folding screen that
provides some privacy from the street.

But it's the salle de bain, or bathroom, that really seals the
deal. It's a cupboard—literally a WC in the purest sense of
the term—a freestanding, prefabricated vinyl-covered wardrobe
unit, circa 1970s, with doors that open to reveal a handbasin and
shelves on one side and a hanging wardrobe for clothes on
the other. It's the sort of bathroom arrangement you might

find in steerage on a cheap cruise liner. The entire front of the cupboard swings 180 degrees around to reveal a tiny dark shower recess with a toilet to one side; you could sit on the loo and shower at the same time if you really wanted to. While my initial reaction is one of horror at the hideousness of the unit, I am also quite amused at the notion of living with such an eccentric amenity. I agree to move in the following Saturday.

My room faces south, and gets the full force of both the midday and afternoon sun. When I open the door on the day of the move, I am almost overwhelmed by the acrid stench of tomcat piss, a smell I have become accustomed to over a lifetime of cat ownership. Obviously Jean and Lisette have been leaving the windows and shutters open in an attempt to air the room before I move in, and the local tomcats have simply taken the opportunity to claim the territory in turn. I throw open the windows and shutters to let in some fresh air before bringing my modest possessions inside. Jock has loaned me some sheets, a sharp knife, an extra pillow and a radio which he assures me will get the French classical music channel and possibly even the BBC World Service. I cannot start putting anything away because everything in the room is covered in a layer of grime—I guess nobody has lived here for months, if not years. Rooms like this, understandably, are not in big demand.

In the late afternoon while I am washing pots and pans I hear a cat fight and rush to the window to catch a glimpse of a ginger and white tomcat with the largest pair of balls I have ever seen. Perhaps his half-starved body accentuates their size, but they appear to be glued to his rear end like two enormous ping pong balls. He turns and scowls at me before stalking off. I have moved into his patch and he is not amused. Normally I am a sucker for stray cats, and will feed any vaguely hungry-looking cat that saunters into my orbit. But these village toms are not to be encouraged with tasty snacks, rather kept at bay, unless I am to be overrun. In fact, two cats pay me a nocturnal visit on my first night—I shout at them and they make a hasty exit, hopefully without having sprayed their trademarks all over the room before waking me. It's not ideal sleeping without fresh air and it's been my lifetime habit to leave the bedroom windows open in the summer, even when I'm not at home. At night the idea of sleeping with the windows closed is claustrophobic, so I rig up a temporary barrier behind the half-closed shutters using a clothes drying rack. It somehow ruins the ambience of the only 'French feature' of what Jock calls 'Mary's Hovel'.

When I was seventeen and planning to move into my first share house I had the most exciting time with my flatmate Kate, buying all the necessary household bits and pieces. We scrounged essential items including linen, towels and even beds and cupboards from our respective parents' homes, but had a lot of fun lay-bying pretty coffee cups, wineglasses and tablecloths. If we had realised that our live-in boyfriends were hellbent on turning our share house into a nonstop party venue with beer and marijuana soirées, we wouldn't have gone to such a lot of trouble. The cups were quickly broken and the idea of domestic bliss completely shattered. Getting set up in my French hovel is similar, except that I will be totally in control of the situation this time and don't anticipate any all-night rave parties.

My new friend Margaret Barwick lends me a soft, pretty Laura Ashley bed quilt in yellow, blue and white, so I can ditch the resident clean but stained lime green chenille coverlet. Margaret also fills the back of my car with an assortment of decorative and practical items including a Provençal-style yellow and blue tablecloth, some long-stemmed wine glasses, white dinner plates, a lamp, a rug and, best of all, some pretty candle holders and a handful of yellow candles. I'm almost set.

Most domestic stoves in France run on bottled gas, and the bottle in the hovel's stove is empty. I need to take it to a garage and swap it for a full one, then somehow connect it to the cooktop. I also need to clean and plug in the fridge, which is filthy, and wipe down every surface before putting things away. This is a sort of nesting, which I always enjoy: making a place like home, giving it a personal stamp, getting it clean, making it pretty. Some people take no pleasure in cleaning away the grunge left behind by previous inhabitants, but I find it strangely satisfying. Making up the bed is the best part. The sheets Jock loaned me are brand new, and with the bedcover and large white pillow cases, I now have a welcoming place to crawl into at night. The room is so small I can't find anywhere to store the old bedding, now folded into plastic garbage bags. I settle on the boot of my car, where they can remain for the next two months without getting in the way.

There are really very few bedrooms I have inhabited on a permanent basis. Two during my childhood and growing up years, a couple of rented houses with friends in my late teens, and then the two bedrooms I have shared with David over the past thirty years. The first of these was in a small sandstone terrace in the city, the second is the light and airy bedroom of our home in Leura, which has two walls of windows looking out to the garden; this has been my bedroom for the past twenty-three years. The difference with the Villefranche bedroom is that it will be my entire living space for at least two months: a bed, a table, three upright chairs, a shoebox-size kitchen and a loo inside a cupboard that I christen the Tardis. I have no television and Jock's radio barely gets even a fuzzy local reception.

But it's mine, totally mine. My own small space to come and go as I please, to sleep and eat and read and have some thinking time. I love it. When I lie on the bed I am literally one-and-a-half steps from the toilet and two steps from the fridge. In Australia there are strict rules about distances between bathrooms and kitchens, but here no such restrictions seem to apply. I delay the first attempt at using the Tardis, dreading the claustrophobic feeling of swinging the revolving door behind me—it's been designed so that you have to close the door or the toilet lid can't be opened. Eventually I can wait no longer, and climb inside the contraption. The toilet is so low that I am practically crouched in a squatting position, and the shower faucet is almost immediately overhead. But it works fine and I can see no ongoing problem as long as I avoid using the loo immediately after showering, when it will have been well doused in water. I place a lamp on the roof of the unit, which has a translucent ceiling, so that I can actually see what I am doing once inside. It helps.

It's fun to fill the fridge with good things to eat and drink, and it's certainly not difficult shopping in this gorgeous village. The wines are superb and very cheap, as is the beer. However, meat at the smart charcuterie is quite expensive—I am shocked to discover that three lamb cutlets set me back more than 30 ff (nearly $8) but I make them last three meals, so it's not too drastic. Cheeses are irresistible although it's hard to make a decision when there are so many varieties unknown to me displayed in the glass cabinet; a camembert and a blue are a good combination. Fruit and vegetables are abundant at this time of year and they are strictly seasonal and generally locally grown, which means they taste real—no keeping produce in cold storage for weeks at a time or gassing or spraying with preservatives. During my first few weeks the strawberries are being harvested, and mounds of brilliant red heart-shaped fruits are on display everywhere, going cheap. They can be eaten as they come, steeped in sugar and red wine, or lightly stewed. Compared with those huge strawberries grown hydroponically in glasshouses, which are often half ripe and woody when sent to market, these are a total taste sensation.

My first two or three evenings alone in Villefranche feel very strange indeed. The late afternoons and early part of the evenings seem to drag interminably. I try and think of things to fill the hours: walking around the village; sitting in the Hotel du Commerce having a couple of beers; planning and preparing a sumptuous dinner; writing postcards to friends and family; or reading whatever English-language book, magazine or newspaper I can lay my hands on. The daytimes are not a problem because I usually drive to St Caprais first thing to check my email on Jock's up-to-date computer, then get caught up in whatever he is planning for the day—generally a drive to a nearby village market followed by lunch somewhere cheap and interesting. My habit then is to wend my way back to Villefranche in the afternoon to have a two-hour siesta. It's the first time in my life that I have ever indulged in afternoon naps: it feels very decadent but delightful. I simply close the timber shutters leaving open the glass windows inside, which allows some airflow but makes the room quite cool and dark; shafts of sunlight force their way through the few cracks where the old shutters don't quite meet. I lie on top of the bed, generally stark naked because the days are overwhelmingly hot, and quickly slip into a carefree but deep sleep. Having no phone and with nobody but Jock knowing my exact location, I am enveloped in a rare sensation of freedom. Nobody can touch me. My afternoon sleep can't be stolen by a phone call or the shrill sound of the fax machine; by a courier banging on the front door delivering yet more work, setting the dog to barking. I am untouchable.

Waking from a daytime sleep, however—especially after having some wine with lunch—is not all that pleasant. Often I have a dry mouth, thick head and a distinct feeling of disorientation. I guzzle down some bottled water, splash my face from the tap and open the shutters to let in the late afternoon sunshine. The hours between now and bedtime have to be filled and I'm finding that yet another new hurdle to leap. For decades my waking hours have been totally filled with nonstop and often frenetic activity. My days flash past too quickly as I race against the clock to accomplish all the set tasks, be they work- or gardening- or family-related. Now six or seven hours stretch ahead of me, and filling them is daunting. It's too late to go off driving around the countryside and too hot in July for walking until well after eight o'clock in the evening, unless it's through the woods in dappled shade. After a large midday meal my energy levels are quite low, and I look for more passive activities. I've never had time to kill and I should be enjoying it. But I don't. I feel flat and rather bored. And irritated with myself for not feeling like doing much at all. I keep thinking here I am in this marvellous place and all I am doing is eating, drinking and sleeping. It's part of an old expectation thing: I should be DOING something. ACHIEVING something. I must somehow let all these feelings go. I am not here to accomplish anything at all, other than just to fall about and be myself, to relax and have some fun. But it's extremely difficult breaking habits of a lifetime.

A chilled beer at the Hotel du Commerce wakes me up properly at 8 pm, then I wander back to the room to make dinner. At home the family would have well and truly finished dinner by now, eating between the ABC news at 7 pm and the current affairs programs as part of a long addiction to the evening news. Here I don't even start peeling a potato until after 8.30, and often don't eat until 9.30 or 10 pm. While the dinner cooks I read the English newspapers, which are delivered to Villefranche a day after publication, and I drink a little chilled rosé. I read every line of the newspaper, except the sport. At home I am a skimmer, reading the lead paragraphs and getting through the entire paper in about twenty minutes. Here I can make the *Times* last for four hours, and be really well informed, if a little out of date.

With some feelings of guilt, I decide to start assembling the yellow and blue fabrics that I bought in Provence to make a cot quilt for the new baby due in eight weeks. I have also bought a book of designs, and cut out the cardboard templates from an old cereal packet. Originally I intended to sew the entire quilt by hand, but Margaret lends me her sewing machine to make the task much faster. The available light is excellent until quite late in the evening—indeed the sun doesn't set before 10 pm—so I can see well enough to work away on the quilt after dinner. I am trying to feel a connection with this unborn child, which is much more difficult to do when we are on opposite sides of the world. My small table is overcrowded with sewing equipment, local travel guides, novels and reference books, plus my computer, giving the impression that the room is the centre of an incredible hive of activity. I cannot seem to escape this image of being fully occupied, no matter where I go.

On the old timber sideboard I've placed a framed photograph of my four little grandsons, one snapped over a year ago showing them tumbling together on a sofa, giggling and being a bit wild. Hamish is staring straight down the lens of the camera, and out of the frame his eyes feel as though they are boring right into me. Looking at the photograph is unbearable, and makes me feel quite weepy. Am I maudlin from too much wine? Am I eating and drinking to excess to compensate for being alone? What am I doing here, so far away from these little ones that I love so much? I turn the photo to the wall and go to bed though I'm not really feeling tired, either physically or mentally.

I know of plenty of people in my age group or even older who are appalled at the idea of becoming grandparents. Nothing could be more instantly aging than accepting the existence of a grandchild, and in some instances these friends and acquaintances simply fail to tell their work colleagues that their families have expanded. It must be our generation's desire to remain forever young and sexually desirable—never to reach middle age and certainly never to become old. Being a grandparent is synonymous with being old, and is definitely off the agenda for many baby-booming women in particular. So many women of my generation didn't start having children until in their thirties—some even in their forties. They don't expect grandchildren until they are well into their sixties. And not one moment sooner! One rather gorgeous forty-eight-year-old divorcee in my circle of acquaintances has threatened to abandon her adult children immediately if they dare to start producing offspring for at least another ten years; she gave birth to her children in her early twenties but the thought that they may repeat her behaviour pattern, and make her a grandmother 'before her time', is anathema.

I became a grandmother at forty-three and by the time I turned fifty there were four little boys in the next generation. Not only did I have no problem accepting my new role as a grandmother, I embraced it wholeheartedly, taking great delight in boring my friends rigid with tales of my adorable grandsons, photos of their antics and news of their progress. One close friend, a fairly staunch Catholic with a large family of her own yet only two grandchildren, eventually became irritated by my constant gloating.

'It's not a competition you know, Mary,' she bleated when I informed her with glee that a fifth grandchild would be born the following September.

I missed out on having grandparents, and I know that as a young child I sorely regretted this loss. My maternal grand-mother was well into her forties when my mother was born, and she died not long after I was born; both my grandfathers died decades previously. My father's mother lived in Melbourne and I never once met her, although I was named after her and almost ten years old when she died. One of the consequences of my father's alcoholism was that he lost all contact with his family. My mother, however, painted wonderful word pictures of her own mother, whom she obviously adored for her gentleness and intelligence, her warmth and frailty. So I spent my child-hood fantasising about having a 'real' grandmother who I imagined somehow seeing me as I played and even watching over me like an invisible guardian. I vividly recall walking down the side pathway of our block of flats and talking to my imaginary grandmother, telling her all about what I was doing and hoping that she would admire me. It was a harmless enough fantasy but tinged with sadness because in my heart of hearts I knew that neither of my grandmothers had known anything about me at all.

My own mother, through the unusual circumstances of her living under the same roof as my growing family, became much more of a grandmother than I think she ever really intended. I know that my children benefited enormously from having this close bond with my mother, and if you asked them now, as they are launching into parenthood themselves, they would all heartily agree. I am therefore determined to be as involved and as important in my grandchildren's worlds as my mother was in the lives of my children. I can't see myself living in the same house as them, although we have all had spells of living together in between their various comings and goings from rental houses to house buying. At one stage we even had four generations squeezed into the house together. Just like in the old French farming families where they somehow all managed to get along—though in a single, very confined living space.

I love the physical aspect of being a grandmother—the unconditional uninhibited hugging and smooching, the way small children clamber onto my hip when I'm cooking or climb into my bed in the middle of the night, even if it is with soggy pyjama pants. The hugging and touching that comes with being close to babies and small children is very powerful, and I really miss it when I am away from them. In the village streets on market day I find myself looking longingly at small children in strollers and wanting to stroke their hair or tickle them, but I know that their parents would probably think me a little odd. I seize upon any opportunity to spend time with children—anyone's children or grandchildren—just to enjoy being around small people. When Jock's neighbours in St Caprais are visited by their daughter from England with two small children in tow, I can't wait to get my hands on them. The day they arrive I offer my babysitting services, hoping they will take advantage of being able to go out together for a meal without the little ones underfoot. They are delighted and organise a dinner out together at the rather upmarket restaurant at Les Arques, but sadly the children have been tucked into bed and are well and truly asleep by the time the adults depart. I keep popping in and checking on them, hoping one might wake and need some grandmotherly cuddles, but they remain soundly sleeping for the entire time I am in charge of them.

I have never wanted to be one of those scone-baking, knitting types of grandmas with my hair in a bun and fluffy slippers. Instead I fancy I am a grandmother who makes the children laugh and scandalises them a little—a saucy sort of irreverent grandmother who pokes fun at conservatism. Just like my mother, I guess!

My physical longing for the little boys and my homesickness is repeated several times over the next few nights, until I start to settle into my new daily routine. Amazingly, after only a week or ten days I begin to feel more at home and quite comfortable. My initial emotions must have been sparked by a feeling of strangeness and alienation, but in time I develop a sense of belonging. Is this normal human behaviour? Perhaps a strategy for surviving in unaccustomed environments? Whatever, I am relieved that I am no longer tearful and depressed. I start to look forward to the evenings of lingering twilight, watching locals and tourists walk past my windows as I sip wine, read, sew and cook. I could easily get used to this.

14

VILLEFRANCHE-DU-PÉRIGORD is classified as an historic bastide town, one of about three hundred similar towns and villages built in the region during the Middle Ages under the joint authority of wealthy landowners and ruling feudal powers. The English were a major presence on and off for centuries in southwest France and they also built bastide towns during periods when they controlled particular regions. The bastides, which were sometimes fortified, were laid out in a rectangular or square grid pattern based around a square with a timber-roofed market hall, often with arcades and archways where other shops were located. The rationale behind the construction of the bastides was to provide a place to trade that had some security; they provided a secure haven for families during a disorderly period when living isolated in the countryside was dangerous, and they also provided a focus for marketing and trading.

Although many of the bastide towns were destroyed during the turmoil of the fourteenth century, some survive to this day in remarkably good condition. Villefranche was founded in 1261 and was one of the English-built bastides. It has fortunately remained less sought after by tourists so it has retained its character—no rows of shops selling tourist trinkets, indeed quite a few of the shops are empty which makes it quiet midweek and in the off season. One exception is the period during autumn when the cèpe (mushroom) season is at its peak.

Villefranche is a focal town for buying and selling cepes and the Saturday market goes mad with people bargaining for these strange-looking but delicious mushrooms gathered in the nearby chestnut and oak woods.

The large, open square has a covered market hall which still has the fixed, swinging metal containers that were once used to measure wheat, corn and other grains. There are four parallel streets running away from the square, barely wide enough for a horse and cart or a car. The cross streets are very narrow indeed, some barely wide enough for a person to walk through. This street and laneway layout was also part of the bastide plan, to eliminate escape routes for marauders on horseback who would be forced to use the wide streets with no way of disappearing down a back alley. The main street has been made one-way and has no footpaths to speak of, but visitors park down one side, against the wall, and the largest of delivery vans and tourist camper vans squeeze between the parked cars and the opposite wall. Side mirrors take quite a battering and as a shopper on foot I feel no more at ease from impending danger than the original villagers. I really have to have my wits about me, listening for cars coming up behind and learning to jump out of the way quickly; heaven knows how more toddlers don't come to grief on the main street. The locals, however, don't even seem in the slightest bit perturbed by the perilous pedestrian conditions. Perhaps they have an inbuilt faith that the cars and trucks will stop before hitting them. I simply can't feel so relaxed about it.

The cool, shady archways fronting the Hotel du Commerce would have originally housed shops and market stalls. There is now a bar and a good restaurant, with comfortably furnished rooms upstairs that have been recently renovated. The Commerce quickly becomes my local watering hole, and I wander in at lunchtime or in the evening for a beer. Within a week of my arrival the barmaid greets me with a wide smile and pours my draught beer without being asked. There is another bar, dark and small, where the locals tend to drink more but I never feel quite as much at home when I venture in there; often a card game, with attendant shouting and gesticulating, is in progress and non-regulars tend to be ignored.

There is a small supermarket in the main street run by a very friendly and helpful young couple, an alimentation and a gourmet deli with prepared dishes such as quiche and couscous as well as superior cheeses and wines. On Saturday and Sunday the owner of the deli seductively positions a huge hotplate in the street outside the front door, cooking either paella piled high with saffron rice and prawns, or a mixed dish of sautéed chicken, herbs and potatoes. The aromas that fill the entire street make passing by without buying very difficult indeed.

The charcuterie in the main street is run by a slender, elegant man named Claude who wears an immaculate floor-length white apron over his butcher's pants. He makes a theatrical production out of serving each and every customer—even small orders like mine—and presenting and wrapping everything beautifully. In France shopping for food is an art form, and housewives prize themselves on thrift and getting good value for money. I am told various anecdotes, including one about a canny woman who points to a joint of meat and asks for its bone, which is virtually given away at no cost. She then asks for the fat from the same joint for rendering down, also sold extremely cheaply. Finally, she decides to buy the meat itself, now much lighter, having been stripped of the weighty bone and outer fat layer, and therefore less expensive. There is also a legendary tale about a woman who visits the same butcher every morning just before lunch when the charcuterie is always crowded with last-minute shoppers. She never has more than just a few centimes tucked in her apron pocket, and ritually begins by denigrating everything in the window display: the lamb looks tough, the pork is too fatty for her taste, and the veal certainly couldn't be fresh. It is her way of saving face, because in the end she buys what she always intended and could afford in the first place—a length of cheap and fatty Toulouse sausage. One day the butcher can take her whingeing and complaining in front of his other customers no longer. As she moves through her diatribe against his display cabinet he suddenly whips a large cleaver from behind his apron, plunges his hand into his groin, and pulls out a grotesque and phallic length of sausage which he seemingly severs from his body in one sharp movement. Horrified, she shrieks and runs from the shop, never to return, patronising the small charcuterie on the square from that day onwards.

I quickly make myself known to the baker, whose wife cheerfully cuts me a half baguette; French bread is wonderful when fresh but becomes stale within twelve hours and leftovers are wasted unless you have a machine that will grate them finely for breadcrumbs. Traditionally, stale bread is used as the filling basis of a rustic garlicky soup and some cooks also use old bread to thicken stocks and stews; otherwise it ends up being fed to the chickens.

Village life is slow and measured. Much of the culture and conversation revolves around food—what's in season, what's worth buying at the market and how it should or could be cooked. Lunch is the most important meal of the day, and it's a time when I love to wander up and down the back streets where the shutters and windows have been thrown open against the summer heat, just so that I can absorb the mingled aromas of a hot lunch being prepared and listen to the sounds of knives and forks clattering against plates and wine glasses being clinked. A cynical friend asks if during my midday rambles I also hear the sound of soap operas blaring from television sets, implying that the villagers now watch television while they eat lunch. But I can only hear the convivial sounds of conversation and laughter, and smell aromas like pommes frites being sautéed.

Most of the permanent village residents appear to be older people, women in particular, who wear blue coverall aprons like a uniform over their day clothes as they go about the morning shopping and cleaning chores. They lovingly tend their pots and tubs of geraniums and begonias; there isn't exactly a competition to create the most splendid display, but there's certainly a great sense of pride in maintaining these lush gardens on narrow balconies and against the front wall of each house. The pots are watered daily, spent blooms are routinely deadheaded, and the area around each display swept spotlessly clean.

The women shop carrying straw baskets and talk together in the street in small huddles, always greeting me with a warm smile and a 'Bonjour Madame' as I also do my morning shopping.

Some engage me in polite conversation about the weather, which I find most encouraging for my faulty French language skills. They have a curious way of saying, 'It's not hot' when it's cold and, 'It's not cold' when it's hot, which causes me some temporary confusion as the words hot and cold are my lifeline in any conversation about the weather. Within weeks I am copying their quirky turn of phrase. During hot summer afternoons and evenings the women also tend to sit outside on their front steps in small groups, to chat and watch the passing parade. Sometimes they sit there for hours—I see them when I am sauntering to the Commerce for a beer, and they are still there when I am going home. Again, they always give me a cheerful greeting or a wave. I have managed to communicate that I am living in the village for two months, and I am locally known as 'the Australian woman'. I begin to feel very much at home.

Most of the houses in the village have exposed creamy stone facades, but they didn't always look like this. Thirty years ago if you had visited Villefranche-du-Périgord it would have seemed grey and drab because the fashion for rendering the stone with 'crépi' earlier in the nineteenth century meant that virtually every building looked the same. Over time this grey concrete render ages to a dirty and depressing shade, and it was only as the English started buying up old houses and restoring them to their former glory that the crépi started to disappear from the scene. Fortunately most of the older style windows and doors have been retained, except in a few instances where modern prefab windows and metal shutters have replaced the old timber. Now, however, Villefranche is protected from modernisation because of its bastide heritage, and it is illegal to make 'improvements' that spoil the ancient appearance of the buildings. Some of the older towns and villages even have their electricity cables running underground so that no poles or wires detract from the mediaeval atmosphere, and television aerials and satellite dishes are by law positioned where they cannot be seen from the street. In Villefranche, however, the dishes that allow people to watch several hundred European television stations are visible everywhere, and there are other modern conveniences like 'hole in the wall' banking and phone boxes that can be used for international calls.

At one end of the village is the old cemetery, surrounded by a high stone retaining wall that fronts the main road on one side. There don't seem to be any really old individual gravestones, as families customarily have a crypt where all the generations are buried together. Some of these family crypts are quite elaborate, taking the form of a small house, with a roof and steps, but most are simple stone structures covered with elaborate china memorial plaques. The family name is at the back of the crypt, and the individual memorial plaques are added after each funeral; some are brightly coloured china pansies with inscriptions. But there are no dates so it's impossible to tell when individuals have died. I am told a story about a violent storm several years back, which flooded the town and caused one side of the cemetery retaining wall to collapse into the main street during the night. In the morning the villagers were horrified to discover that a recent grave had cascaded open, with the coffin rolling out leaving the body exposed. The worst part was that instead of being clad in his best suit, as is the custom, the deceased was roughly wrapped in an old sheet. His widow evidently kept the suit and sold it, and it was many months before the poor woman was brave enough to show her face in the main street again. It proved to me that even in these sophisticated times of satellite television connection and electronic banking, many of the old customs die hard. So to speak.

There are quite a few retired English couples living in Ville-franche, and there seems to be a general tolerance of such invaders. Indeed, this part of France is renowned for its racial tolerance, which I suspect must be the result of hundreds—perhaps thousands—of years of having to adapt to invaders of one sort or another. The only groups who appear to be univer-sally disliked are the Germans—many of the locals endured German occupation during the Second World War—and Dutch tourists who are considered very parsimonious. Apparently, Dutch visitors come in campervans and bring all their own food and wine, contributing nothing to the local economy. Even if they rent gites they do all their own cooking without shopping at the markets or dining in the cafés; in some villages where a dozen or more Dutch families are holidaying, a huge truck comes across from Holland selling food and beer. It is greatly frowned upon.

The Parisians are also generally disliked for their arrogance, whereas the British, if they are friendly and attempt to assimi-late by learning the language, are much more warmly welcomed. My favourite local story involves two such Parisians, a couple of gay men who arrived several years ago to open a small antique shop in the main street and to live in a cottage on the outskirts of the town. Within a few months they managed to alienate their neighbour—a well-loved farmer—by complaining bitterly about his rooster which woke them up far too early in the morning for their Parisian tastes. When the farmer refused to silence his bird, the couple took their complaints further, initially to the local gendarmerie then to the Palace of Justice in Bordeaux. With a good lawyer on their side they won the case, however the court awarded a fine of only 10 ff against the farmer to symbolise its disgust at the proceedings. The next weekend the farmers and villagers banded together and staged a protest street parade of children and animals. Cows and chickens, goats and horses, ducks, geese and sheep all paraded down the main street to the beat of drums and the clanging of cymbals, passing slowly and ceremoniously in front of the antique shop. The children wore T-shirts printed with the slogan, 'Ne touche pas à mon coq', which loosely translates as 'Hands off my rooster', and at the end of the parade they gathered in the ancient village square where a jaunty local band had been hired to play music. There was much singing, dancing and general merriment while the Parisian antique dealers peered out nervously from behind their shutters. The story was well covered in the local media and even made it to the evening news in Paris—the ultimate humiliation. Surprisingly, four years later they are still living in Villefranche, though keeping a much lower profile and never complaining publicly about a thing.

There is a strong feeling of community within the township, with everyone throwing their full support behind events like village fêtes and repas (feasts), brocantes (antique fairs) and fundraising evenings organised for the football club or the Pompiers, which is a group of civilian volunteers who perform vital services such as firefighting, ambulance and rescue operations. In my first week there is a village meal organised to raise money for the football team, and Jock comes over to join in. The poster bills it as a 'Paella Géant' which indeed it is—a paella pan about four metres across that starts being prepared about midday for serving at 9 pm. The smell of garlic, saffron and seafood fills the entire square, and tables are set out in the hall for several hundred people. For 100 ff ($25) patrons get a five-course meal: a rich soup of garlic and bread; a rough country pâté with fresh bread; the paella piled with prawns, chicken and spicy sausage; followed by cheese, then glazed apple tart. The red wine is compris (included in the price) and as each bottle is finished another appears as if by magic. There is coffee and the local pear liqueur, eau de vie, which is about as potent as any alcohol I've ever tasted. Strictly speaking distilling liquor is highly illegal, but it is such a strong tradition in these parts that nobody dares enforce it. Eau de vie can be made from any fruit that can be fermented but plum, pear and apple are the most popular. I remember this stuff from my birthday lunch: one tiny glass of this firewater is more than enough.

Later in the evening—after three-and-a-half hours of wining and dining—we retire to the tables and chairs of the Hotel du Commerce in the square for more coffee. It's nearly midnight when the children are each given a candlelit lantern to carry, and are led with music in a parade down the main street; despite the late hour, it's a village tradition to include children in most social occasions. As they return, there's a small but pretty fire-works display against the facade of the old stone church. People are still drinking and talking and children are still running excitedly around the square as I wander off to bed at nearly 1 am.

From my bedroom near the main street I can usually hear if there's a village celebration or a more sombre occasion like the church bells ringing incessantly for a funeral service. The most alarming sound that intrudes on my life, however, is that of the siren that calls the Pompiers into action. It's akin to a wartime air raid siren and it can go off at any time of the day and night, though somehow three o'clock in the morning seems to be the most popular time slot. The Pompiers are a group of highly respected civilians who have been professionally trained for all the rescue functions normally performed by ambulance, police rescue and fire brigade. They have become a vital resource in remote and rural areas where there are no government funds for such essential services. They deal with every imaginable emergency, from car accidents to floods and fires, to heart attacks and babies being born before they reach the hospital, or to simple domestic crises situations, like wasp nests stuck in the chimneys. The force is drawn from a cross-section of men in the community, from the main street butcher to the real estate agent, and when they need to be rallied to attend some local disaster, the sirens sound the alarm. Each ring seems interminable, and there are different numbers of rings according to the type of emergency: one long ring means a car accident, two long rings means a heart attack, and so on, so that the men, as they scramble into their uniforms, at least have a vague idea of what they are about to deal with.

The Pompiers siren is so frightfully loud that the first time it explodes through my bedroom window I am convinced World War Three has begun. My heart thumping in my throat, I run to see what is going on, but all seems amazingly calm outside. Then the alarm rings again and I hear sounds of cars starting up in the laneways around the village. It isn't until the following day when I ask around that I am told about the Pompiers, and right through the summer my sleep is frequently shattered by these sirens. The work and dedication of these unpaid community servicemen is taken very seriously, but I sense something slightly comical in the way they go about their business. They're a little like Dad's Army, or some of our less active bushfire brigades who perform magnificently when there is a crisis, but seem also to spend a lot of time drinking beer and playing with their equipment on quiet Saturday afternoons during the non-fire-fighting season.

Over time various people tell me anecdotes about the Pompiers, including Jock's friends Carole and Bob who had to call them one weekend when they discovered a huge nest of angry wasps in the chimney of their youngest son's bedroom. Lights flashing, the Pompiers truck appeared several hours later in their driveway, disgorging half a dozen uniformed but ill-equipped men. Being hospitable, Bob offered them a glass of wine, which they readily accepted. After an hour of drinking and chatting they decided to deal with the wasp nest, but realised they had no ladder to gain access to the roof, and no bucket to catch the nest when it was dislodged. Having borrowed these items from Carole they proceeded to free the nest from the chimney, and carry it outside where it was destroyed. They returned to the kitchen table for several more rounds of vin, then screamed off at speed in their truck, flattening the expensive borrowed galvanised bucket as they departed.

Without the Pompiers to help out with road accidents, however, the already alarming death and serious injury statistics in southwest France would be even worse. In time I learn to ignore the shrieking siren, rolling over and going straight back to sleep.

Villefranche is alive with stray cats, most of them very thin and certainly not desexed. My initial decision to ignore them comes undone one morning when a handsome but lean young tabby tomcat leaps through the window and starts purring so loudly I can barely hear the radio. I scrounge in the fridge to find him some bits to eat, and give him a saucer of milk. He is ostentatiously grateful, rubs my legs and purrs loudly before settling in the middle of the bed to clean himself and sleep. I name him Pierre the Pussy and he becomes a regular visitor, but the last thing I want to do is to make a cat dependent on me as I am staying for such a short period. Pierre is a real character, he hurls himself through the window and straight onto my bed with great enthusiasm or tries to play with my feet as I sit at the table reading or writing. However, like most cats that have not been handled routinely by people from kittenhood, he doesn't quite know how to play without inflicting pain: he grabs my leg and sinks his claws and teeth in, then is amazed when I shriek and leap to my feet. Thankfully Pierre doesn't stay all day; after a catnap he takes off and I regularly see him in the village. When the market is being held on Saturday mornings he lies beside the fish stall sunning himself, obviously waiting for a discarded treat. He also hangs around the Hotel du Commerce restaurant at lunch and dinner time. Friends who have supper there one evening report that a friendly village cat swung from their tablecloth until he was given a piece of steak. I ask them to describe this freeloader, and it matches Pierre to a whisker. It is reassuring that he has plenty of other sources of food—I am just one of the many suckers on his daily rounds. Within two weeks another cat arrives, a desexed female and obviously also very well fed. She is much more demanding than Pierre but just as affectionate and I weaken. So I now have two regular feline visitors who some-times arrive at the same time and hiss and snarl at each other at first, but settle to drink saucers of milk side by side.

One day when I am in the phone box calling David, Pierre sees me through the glass doors and miaows loudly to be let in. I open the doors and he enters, purring and miaowing so vigorously that David in far-off Queensland can hear him clearly down the phoneline. After ten minutes of rubbing my shins he becomes impatient—he wants me to take him back to my room and feed him—and stretches up and bites me hard on the shin. I quickly turf him out and he sits scowling at me through the glass, then stalks off before I finish talking. Several weeks later Pierre arrives at my windowsill with a third cat, a large, black desexed male who tentatively sits on the outside, peering in. I am determined not to start feeding yet another stray cat but he seems quite happy anyway, purring and watching us inside while having a good view of the action out on the street. The village cats are terrified of dogs, probably with good reason, and they never seem totally relaxed, even when inside my flat. They are always on the lookout for a predator and I suppose the other, wilder tomcats must also be a threat, so their life is never really carefree like our own domesticated moggies.

Towards the end of my two months in Villefranche I have to accept that I now have three cats who love to pop in for a visit, for a saucer of milk, some dry biscuits and a comfortable place to carry out their cleaning ritual and snooze. One day I return from the shops and find all three of them asleep on my bed. It feels very much like home.

15

FRENCH RURAL COMMUNITIES live for the summer. When the crops fill the fields and the grapes are swelling on the vine and twilights are long and warm, living outdoors is a delight. From June until September the southwest region reaches its highest population, with summer holiday-makers coming from the UK and other parts of Europe to savour all the pleasures it has to offer. August is possibly the peak month, when the French and English have their main school and business holidays, and every weekend is alive with cele-brations, antique fairs, feasts and communal parties. It's a time of nonstop eating and drinking.

Among Jock's circle of friends, summer is always a busy social-ising time, with part-time residents arriving in dribs and drabs and getting into the swing of it. There are plenty of activities to keep visitors entertained, both during the day and into the evening. You could easily find something new and interesting to do every day, if your stamina was up to the pace. I certainly did my best to keep up, trying not to miss out on anything.

Near Frayssinet-le-Gélat is a body of water grandly known as the Plan d'Eau. It is a manmade lake, which feeds into two smaller streams, one of which was originally used to run the local millhouse. During the summer months the water outlets are closed marginally so that the lake fills to capacity, making it a refreshing swimming area shaded by huge plane trees. There is a bar–café that opens during this balmy period to serve cold drinks, ice creams and simple lunches to families enjoying the cooling waters of the lake. On the way back from market or sight-seeing, Jock and I call in for a pression, or draught beer, and are always warmly greeted by the cheerful barmaid, Christine. We are regulars, often stopping for a light lunch of salad or omelette. On Friday and Saturday evenings there are also simple meals at the Plan d'Eau, the best being the eccentric combination of moules et frites (mussels and chips); although the regional cuisine is extensive and varied, the locals also enjoy a wide range of specialities from other parts of France and Europe, and this one comes from the Belgian border area, and is simply a huge bowl of steaming mussels accompanied by an equally huge bowl of hot, crisply fried chips. Together with bread and beer or red wine, it's a meal not to be missed and is surprisingly rich and filling—we are groaning by the time we make it to the bottom of the bowls. There are also spaghetti nights and other evenings where the locals come to eat steak or chops and frites and play boules well into the evening. The tranquil setting, with the water sparkling and the trees spreading their cooling shade and the children paddling on the edges, is like a dappled Monet painting.

This time of year also means the village streets are blocked off regularly for antique markets as well as book and junk fairs.

The standard of goods on sale varies according to the name given to the occasion: 'brocante' implies an antique sale; 'vide grenier' is an attic or boot sale; 'troc' means to barter and this usually also indicates a junk sale; while 'salon du livre' indicates a book, magazine and art print sale. Sometimes the fairs are a little bit of all these various things mixed in together, with some gorgeous antique furniture and bric-à-brac lumped together with all sorts of rubbishy goods of little value. It's a treasure trove for those who have somewhere to put what they are buying. All I can think about is the impossibility of trying to get goods back to Australia and so am constantly in the position of resisting temptation. It's very frustrating.

The first sale day I attend is a troc at Duravel, about twenty minutes drive from Villefranche on the other side of the Lot River. The village square and surrounding streets have been taken over by literally hundreds of small stalls, some on tables but more often simply laid out on old sheets or blankets on the ground. By custom each household in the village is entitled to set up a stall, and it's a great way of clearing out unwanted junk and making a few centimes into the bargain. Some of these fairs discourage professional dealers or traders who compete with the village people, and some welcome them to add a bit of glamour to the occasion. It's a bit of a free-for-all and keen buyers start arriving early in the morning to snaffle up the best bargains. We arrive mid-morning and the atmosphere is rich. Caravans serving steaming black coffee and warm croissants compete with beer and wine stands for custom. I am overwhelmed by the sheer number of articles on display, from some quite splendid pieces of furniture, china and glassware to stuff normally relegated to the rubbish bin. Who would want to buy a broken saucer or a cracked teapot minus the lid, or a filthy rubber doll with wild eyes and no arms? I am drawn to the stalls selling old garden tools and agricultural paraphernalia, such treasures that I wish I could load them into a container and take them back to Australia. There are brass backpack drums used for spraying gardening chemicals such as arsenic during the last century—I have seen pictures of them over many years of research in books about garden history. Some of them have been polished and others are crying out for restoration. There are wicker baskets and trays for gathering and drying the harvest, glass bells for covering seedlings to protect them from frosts, all manner of old pruning tools and spades, as well as forks made from willow. I am enraptured.

I am also drawn to the collections of tin-lined copper cooking pots that were commonly used in kitchens all over France. They are incredibly heavy and would be impossible to carry home—I imagine myself with cooking pots slung over my shoulder trying to board the plane at Paris. There are piles of beautiful antique linen: bedspreads, sheets, pillowcases, curtains and delicately embroidered white nightgowns that look as though they were never worn apart perhaps from a few brief moments before being removed on the wedding night. Seeing all the bric-à-brac of everyday living from the past gives me a fascinating insight into the local way of life.

In my real life I seldom have time to browse in antique shops and I rarely, if ever, stop to rifle through boxes of unwanted household items at a garage sale. I have many friends who regularly attend auctions and open days and regard trawling for bargains as a splendid way to while away their weekends. My lifestyle dictates that the weekends are for early morning shopping and cooking up large family feasts, and spending whatever few hours I can spare to weed my garden or tend the vegetable patch. I usually allow some time for grandmotherly play with the little ones, although I also often work at my computer over the weekend, trying to meet outstanding deadlines or to get ahead on projects. In the end my weeks and weekends often blur into a flurry of work and commitments. Therefore leaping around these charmingly different flea markets and seeing what's on offer is a rare treat, even if I am not in the position to spend any money.

Although the village antique and jumble sales are a great way of picking up interesting local furniture and household goods, a lot of the items on sale are also ridiculously overpriced when you consider how junky they are. It's almost as if the owners don't really want to part with them. On the other hand, some items are extremely cheap—they would be considered an absolute bargain in an Australian antique stall, and I spend several hours, like everyone else, peering and fossicking among the collections of fascinating articles. The troc is also an opportunity for socialising, seeing friends and being seen, and at Duravel we link up with various members of the gang including retired English photographer Claude, who lives in a beautifully restored millhouse at Frayssinet-le-Gélat; Danny, who is also English and rents his beautiful farmhouse to holidaymakers in the summer; and Anthony, an escapee from the world of high finance who is also in the throes of restoring a stone house and therefore definitely in the market for bargains. Surprisingly, he buys an expensive and totally impractical addition to his new household, a beautiful antique slide projector, possibly more than one hundred years old, but in full working order. He doesn't quite know what he will do with it, but like a lot of market shoppers he just can't resist certain treasures. Jock buys a chipped bowl for 15 ff and is delighted. We decide to meet back at the Pomarède restaurant run by Madame Murat for a simple but weighty five-course lunch. So there goes the afternoon.

Over the next eight to ten weeks there is a market at a different village or township virtually every weekend, and I learn to be quite discriminating about those which are worth visiting and those which are a waste of time. Like most visitors I regard them as the highlight of the week. Nearby Loubejac, with its wonderfully ancient church and village green, hosts a memorable brocante with goods of a quality and price that would easily allow a newcomer to furnish a house and equip it with all manner of household goods very cheaply. I weaken and buy a stylish pastis water bottle for 35 ff and a pair of weird earrings in the shape of cat's heads. Very sixties and rather naff. While we watch various acquaintances exploring the stalls, Jock and I have a beer followed by a mouth-watering baguette stuffed with spicy sausages. The weather is perfect, the setting is bliss and I feel completely happy and at home in this foreign village watching the fun of the fair. It's intriguing comparing purchases and looking at other people's discoveries. Jan and Philippe find a magnificent gilded picture frame and I see Danny on the way home with a classic wrought iron light fitting that he is planning to mount in his downstairs hallway. Jock buys a couple of aluminium gravy boats for 10 ff and is happy as a sandboy.

The grandest of the brocantes is in the popular bastide township of Monpazier, displayed in the elegant square surrounded by cafés and upmarket tourist shops. By this time Jock's gorgeous blonde stepdaughter Claudia has arrived on her honeymoon from America, with her new and slightly bedazzled young husband Michael. She and I fall upon the treasures on offer, staggered at the quality and comparatively low price of the china and glassware, the antique furniture, the books, paintings, prints, carpets and kitchenware. I discover a linen stall with perfect white handmade nightdresses, and buy several as presents for my daughter and daughters-in-law back home. Claudia is also into 'linens' as the Americans call them, and while Michael and Jock sit patiently in a café sipping beer, we dash back and forth with our purchases. After an hour or so even I am worn to a frazzle, but Claudia is just getting into her stride. It's a shoppers' paradise, and very seductive.

The largest secondhand sale of the season is at Cazals, a village about twenty minutes from Villefranche that dates back to the twelfth century. Cazals has a handsome square and a network of old back streets and narrow lanes and its fair has so many stalls that it is impossible to take it all in. Whereas once I tried looking at virtually every item on offer, by now I find I am incapable of absorbing it all. I wander through the square and around a massive arched street that is crammed with displays, and realise I have lost the desire to buy anything much at all. It's the same sort of feeling that often overwhelms me at home in supermarkets and department stores. I am suffering from object overload. I am always attracted to kitsch, however, and Cazals has more than its fair share of hideous items including clocks in the shapes of horses, ashtrays that are women's breasts and tasteless statues of black people that are either moneyboxes or cocktail stands. Some sculptures made by a local 'artist' are beyond belief both in their concept and clumsy execution. I cannot resist a pair of chubby baby legs, obviously moulded from a child's plastic doll, that have been painted blue and sit, torso-less, on a coffee table—perfect for the outdoor bar of my new friends Miles and Anne, who are also into collecting ugly and somewhat offensive objets d'art.

Miles and Anne are relative newcomers to the scene, arriving every August from their smart townhouse in London for six weeks or more. Their rambling house and garden in Frayssinet-le-Gélat is not their first holiday home here, but they have only been in Jock's friendly circle for a couple of years. Unlike some of the other part-time residents they have made the effort to speak French, and employ several people to help them with gardening and renovating, so they are well liked in the village. Miles is a most unlikely character for me to get along with, being English and male, for a start, which has often been a bit of a problem for someone as irreverent as me. A Cambridge graduate, with all the baggage it carries, he works as an executive in the mining industry and has links to Australia that involve the exportation of uranium from our shores. Shock horror. At our first meeting I exclaim with delight that I have probably been involved in more than one greenie protest against his various export operations, but he shrugs this off with good grace. He turns out to be a charming man with a sense of humour akin to my own and it's a good lesson for me in learning to put aside staunchly held political positions and get along with people whose company I would normally shun.

Anne is a talented artist and potter who somehow manages her handful of a husband with good humour—for Miles is a bit of a party animal, who loves long lunches and dinners and any occasion where drinks can be served liberally. Anne has great plans for their beautiful, wild garden. She is quite knowledge-able about plants and appreciates my help with ideas on ways to get her untamed woodland garden established. Yet another convert to mulching under my belt. Miles and Anne usually bring a team of their oldest and dearest friends along for part of the summer holiday. Mostly ex-Cambridge mates and their wives, many of Indian origin, they are a highly entertaining and witty bunch when they all get together. We enjoy some memor-able outdoors summer lunches and curry feasts while they are in residence, making it little more than one long summer party. Suddenly I spy them and their assorted friends and houseguests having a beer in the café over the road and before long we are joined by most of the others who have turned out for the Cazals fair.

Frayssinet-le-Gélat also has a vide grenier and it's a real mixed bag of delights. Here I again encounter Anne, who finds a handsome old tin hip bath that she tells me she'll convert into a giant ice bucket to set up beside the bar at their numerous drinks parties on the terrace. This time I resist making a purchase and we all repair to Miles and Anne's for drinks, which is the beginning of my downfall. Miles insists that everyone around him should be having a good time, preferably with a glass in their hand. He is making martinis, not my normal tipple, as beer on a hot summer day is my drink of preference. But I suddenly find myself clutching an ice cold martini, one hundred per cent gin, with the vermouth sprayed lightly over the chilled surface from a perfume bottle. It's delicious and I have a second one, followed by a glass of champagne and some white wine. We enjoy a late lunch of salads, bread and cheese and continue talking and laughing and drinking wine well into the mid afternoon.

Without giving it a second thought, I jump into my car and head back to Villefranche to sleep off the excesses of the day. As I am driving towards the Dordogne border an oncoming car flashes its lights at me, but I ignore the warning. Suddenly I see the reason—the gendarmes are out in force and they are waving me over to the side of the road. The rest is history. I have never been breathalised before and certainly at home in Australia I would never, ever consider driving home after a long, boozy lunch. But here everyone drinks at lunchtime and drives home and I have been stupidly lulled into an unrealistic false sense of security.

Back at the station I am found to be 'just over' the limit and am given an on-the-spot fine of 600 ff and told I can pick my car up after four hours. I am driving on my Australian licence and luckily therefore have no points deducted. I can't help but think I have escaped very lightly indeed. At home I would have automatically lost my licence, would have had to make a court appearance and would have been gleefully written up in the local papers. Here I am given a relatively small fine and offered a lift home by the boys in blue (which I decline). I feel chastened and terribly ashamed at my irresponsible behaviour. I slink back to my room to assess my situation. Late in the evening I walk the five kilometres to the car and drive nervously back to Villefranche as the sun is setting.

The gang reacts to my 'misdemeanour' (the actual word written on the gendarmes' receipt for my fine) with surprise and nervous amusement. I almost become the local hero because I am the first one to ever be caught and fined for drink driving. However I notice a sudden restraint emerging at lunch and dinner times, and sense that generally fewer glasses of wine are being consumed. Main roads are being avoided in favour of trips home through the woods, and suddenly people are teaming up to travel to parties in groups with a 'designated' driver. While the incident certainly does not result in general sobriety, it has given some friends among my circle food for thought. Cynics claim that it would never have happened after one of the St Caprais lunches in the restaurant across the road from Jock's, because the gendarmes are careful not to dampen local businesses by arresting customers for drink driving. All I know is that I will be drinking a lot less if I have to drive, and maybe that's not such a bad thing after all.

There's an irony in the fact that I have been spending so much of my French retreat drinking beer and wine when my young life was so painfully damaged by the excessive use of alcohol by both my parents. The terrible fights in my family, the infidelities and even the attempted and successful suicides can be clearly linked to alcohol abuse. Yet drinking is a part of life that I really enjoy. I love the taste of it, and I love the effect of a couple of glasses of reasonable wine, and I certainly love drinking wine with good food. The French have a very relaxed attitude to drinking, and wine is considered a basic necessity of life—like bread and milk—and is therefore not heavily taxed. The French drink wine every day with meals—both at lunch and at dinner—but they certainly don't drink to get drunk. They just have a couple of glasses of wine and think nothing more about it. You rarely, if ever, see a drunk person around the villages and towns of rural France; there are always a few alcoholics hanging around the squares in the larger cities, but drunks are still relatively inconspicuous compared to other major cities of the world.

When I was working as a young journalist in Sydney, drinking at lunchtime was the norm. We did our interviews in the morning, drank two or three schooners of beer with a sandwich or a pie in the pub at lunchtime, then went back to the office and wrote up our articles for our daily or weekly deadlines. Looking back, I have no idea how we functioned at all, with our bellies full of beer and our brains thick with its numbing effects. Yet it was an accepted part of the journalistic lifestyle, and I can appreciate how my parents were both so easily sucked into regarding alcohol as a vital lubricant in the creative process. When I started working as a freelance writer from home my children were little and those bad lunchtime habits were quickly abandoned—although I did frequently continue to enjoy a cold beer at the end of the day, as a reward and as a way of winding down during that frantic time of evening when children are at their most fractious and the dinner needs to be cooked. For years, when we were strapped for cash, I made my own home-brewed beer, which was quite a lethal drop. One bottle was more than enough to get me through the evening.

Here in France I feel there's something a little bit wicked and self-indulgent about drinking wine with lunch, but because I am in the mood to let my hair down I am loving every minute of it. Deep in my heart I suspect that I could very easily go the same way as my mother, but somehow I seem to manage a greater level of self control. Mum always said that she drank to block out the sadness and trouble in her life, but I realise now that this rationale was just a convenient excuse for not facing the real issues. Alcoholism generally starts quite innocently as a daily ritual then develops into a bad habit, then an addiction that escalates to major social, physical and mental health problems. I am acutely aware of this, having lived with it virtually every day of my life. I am determined it will never happen to me. I enjoy drinking and I intend to continue enjoying it for as long as I can, but I don't intend to allow it to rule my life.

I hope I'm not kidding myself.

16

As a journalist, from a large journalist family, the daily business of keeping on top of the news and maintaining constant communication with people around me has always been a vital part of my existence. Back home, never a day passes that I don't read the newspaper from front to back, watch at least three or four television editions of the news and listen to several more news broadcasts on the radio. I talk to the members of my immediate family every day—often more than once—and we get together for meals or outings at least two or three times a week. I am also a keen reader, preferring to cuddle up in bed with the latest book on the top ten bestseller list than to watch a television drama or serial.

Travelling always poses problems in the area of communication, and to survive as an obsessive news junkie it's a matter of linking into whatever communication resources you can find, be they international news such as CNN or Sky News on a hotel television, or international editions of newspapers.

Travelling to India always means forgetting about news for a week or two. Once we leave Delhi and the comfort of a large hotel, there is no further possibility of getting information about the rest of the world, especially after the trek actually begins. There is something rather interesting about being so far removed from all the troubles of the world, it's as though you are living in a state of suspended animation. Everything just stops for a while and nothing that's happening in the outside world seems to matter. And what you don't know doesn't hurt you. You can't be worried about plane crashes and cyclones and terrorism when you are walking along one of the most ancient goat tracks in the world, surrounded by glorious snow-capped mountain peaks.

Lying at night in my tent, when we have reached the highest point of the trek and are at least five long days walk from the nearest electric cable or telephone, I am always struck by an exhilarating sense of isolation and separation. I would hate to live like this on a permanent basis, but being elevated beyond the chaos of daily news for a few days is really quite invigorating. When I get back to Mussoorie after the long walk I always manage to track down an English-language newspaper with as much determination as I track down my first cold beer. I gradually get back into the ways of the world, and by Delhi I am up-to-date with international events. Australia is rarely, if ever, mentioned in the news unless it's in relation to sport, as it was during the Olympics, or when there's a cricket test match which is, of course, the national Indian obsession. Otherwise Australia is an invisible place. David and my daughter Miriam tell me snippets of local goings on when I call reverse charges from an Indian phone box, but that's about it.

Once I get to France I am confident I will be better informed, and certainly Jock is well set up in the area of information technology. He has a newish computer with email, and a separate phone line, a radio with the BBC World Service and a television that gets both American and English international news channels. However I don't like to monopolise his equipment so for the first three or four weeks, before I move to Villefranche, I only have telephone conversations with home twice and I only catch brief snippets of the news, generally in the mornings before we start our busy day of socialising. Jock buys the *Sunday Times* every Monday morning, a good read except that half the magazine inserts have been left out for the long trip to France. And it's always a day late—in fact all the English papers arrive a day or so late and from a journalist's point of view, old news is stale news. But I am so desperate for the feel of newsprint between my fingers, that I will buy any English language newspaper and read every article, except the business and sport. The English newspapers are also very expensive here, costing up to 25 ff (more than $6) for a paper that would cost 45p ($1.80) in its own country. The number of English holidaymakers during the summer means most of the papers are represented—the *Times*, the *Guardian*, the *International Herald Tribune*, the *Telegraph* and the *Independent*. I have a go at all of them, but end up opting for the *Times*, despite its conservative political leanings, because the arts and news magazine supplements have more interesting articles.

When I finally move to Villefranche I find myself completely cut off from the outside world, without television or international radio or phone. I have an aversion to mobile phones and have never succumbed to having one at home, in spite of the fact that there is a lot of pressure to carry one in my line of work. I rather enjoy being the odd one out, especially when other people's phones ring at inopportune moments. It makes me feel quite smug. So despite various friends suggesting that I simply buy a mobile to use while in France, I resist the temptation. I realise it would be easy and convenient, but the idea of being able to be contacted wherever I might be, whatever I might be doing, certainly does not appeal. I am enjoying the escape from being 'on call' too much to allow a mobile phone to come between me and independence.

I have exhausted Jock's supply of novels and for the first time I feel adrift in the world. It's a strange and rather unsettling feeling. I am anxious to keep in touch with home as my daughter-in-law Lorna's pregnancy progresses and as David is now filming in Queensland. There is no phone line into the little apartment, so even if I felt inclined to have a connection put in it would be very costly. Without a phone connection, of course, I can't get hooked up to the Internet and therefore I can't communicate via email. In any event, the five-year-old laptop which I carted from Australia with a view to writing letters and sending messages home is now obsolete, unable to cope with the software provided by the Internet service providers in France. The problem is that the laptop only takes floppy discs while the software needed to set up an email link is installed with CD roms, so I am unable to get it working even on someone else's phone line. Every day I drive over to Jock's at St Caprais and check my email messages on his computer, then quickly take in some international news on the television. Before leaving Australia I thought I had finished with the manuscript of my huge gardening book, but now the publishers are wanting me to add some lines of text to several entries. Jock's computer can't read the attachments they are sending me, so I have to ask them to send it by snail mail. It is all very frustrating.

With no new books to read I have become totally dependent on my English-language newspapers. Normally I can read a newspaper in half an hour or so, but now I am making them last for hours, poring over every word right down to the television programs that I won't be watching. Jock's old radio gets only fuzzy reception of France Music if I balance it on the windowsill with the aerial poking into the street. It is a marvellous radio station, playing fantastic concerts and music ranging from classics to opera and jazz. But it is also the most intensely irritating station because the announcers love the sound of their own voices and there is more talking about music than actually playing it. I try and concentrate on what they're saying, to help improve my French, but at the end of the day I am hungry for music, for familiar sounds of arias and symphonies and concertos. Even more infuriatingly, they have a tendency to actually stop a piece of music, often mid-climax, and start discussing it in depth. Some of the announcers even sing along with the music or the lyrics, warbling just slightly off mike, producing an effect that has me almost screaming in frustration. Several times I desperately want to throw the radio out on to the street, such is my fury. But it's Jock's radio, and without it I will be living in a world of silence.

Eventually I manage to scrounge some novels from the libraries of various friends, nothing up-to-date but some familiar authors and some I've even read before. But I don't care, I just need words to massage my lonely moments. I take care to write a list of who has lent me what book, knowing that otherwise I will be tearing my hair out when the time comes to send everything back to its rightful owner.

During this period I also stumble across an infuriating

English-language newspaper designed for non-French residents. Called the *News*, the line under the masthead says, 'For lovers of France', but the contents totally contradict this point of view. It's little more than a whinge sheet, with articles emphasising all the negative aspects of living in France, from an English perspective. There are columns and features on how to beat the system, to play the French at their own game, make the most of pensions and retirement funds coming into the country from offshore, and overcome all sorts of bureaucratic problems that must drive the English potty. There are several pompous columns from middle-aged men who, from the photos accompanying their by-line, obviously love one thing in particular about France: their bright faces and rheumy eyes indicate they like to imbibe, in true journalistic fashion. The newspaper is a waste of time and I totally avoid it after thumbing through one or two editions.

By now my inability to understand or speak French very well is becoming frustrating. People said before I left, 'You'll pick it up in no time,' but that simply isn't how things have panned out. Mixing with so many English-speaking people has meant that I don't really get much practice listening to or speaking French, except when I am shopping or strolling around Villefranche. I can get by quite adequately at the presse (newsagency); station service (garage); bureau de poste (post office); supermarché (supermarket) and certainly I have no problems communicating clearly in restaurants and cafés. I can talk weather and in very simple terms about general events—the hunting season or the mushroom season or the walnut season. However, anything more complex and I'm totally stumped. I have done all the right things—listened to French radio stations, especially the news; read the front page of French newspapers; translated posters and flyers sent out to publicise community events, and listened and listened and listened to conversations. My vocabulary has certainly expanded dramatically, and if I were to sit down and make a list of words that I now comprehend and can pronounce, it would run into the hundreds. But stringing them together is another matter altogether. I really need some formal French lessons, but language classes simply don't exist in this area. I find that I can understand the very basics of French conversation when spoken by an English person, because they tend to speak slowly and their accent is probably more attuned to my own ear. However when a French person responds in the course of the conversation, I am completely out of my depth.

A lot of my problem is concentration, combined, I suspect, with laziness and a brain slightly diminished by age and too much good living. When shopping I have fallen into the bad habit of automatically looking at the cash register for the total instead of listening to the total as given by the salesperson. To remedy this situation I teach myself the numerical words, and repeat them out loud every day, several times over. In the supermarket I then listen intently when the woman at the checkout tells me my total, and work out what it means before quickly double-checking the answer by looking at the cash register window. It sometimes takes a minute for me to work it out, but I stop feeling embarrassed about holding up the queue momentarily. After a few weeks this discipline starts to work, and I can finally understand even ridiculously complicated numbers such as ninety-nine, or quatre-vingt-dix-neuf, which translates as four times twenty plus ten plus nine.

In time I manage to teach myself some basic skills, such as using a French-language automatic teller machine, writing out cheques to pay bills in French, and working out the times, dates and venues for various social events publicised on posters. However if I need something accomplished over the phone, I must ask for serious help from a fluent French speaker.

My only French female friend is Lucienne, an elegant woman in her mid seventies, and an old and close chum of the Barwicks who has taken warmly to their motley band of friends. Lucienne is a widow and her late husband was English, which is quite unusual in this region. She lived most of her married life in an old and rambling château at Loubejac, which in keeping with French inheritance laws was sold after her husband's death. She now lives in a traditional stone house with a spacious garden at Pomarède, and is a perfect example of the traditional French hostess and cook. Although her children and grandchildren live in Paris, Lucienne has them to stay for lengthy periods during the summer holidays. She is an active and good-humoured grandmother, taking them swimming and horse riding and feeding them sumptuous meals. She has taken the English-speaking community under her wing, like a French hen, and everyone loves an invitation to dine with her because of the way she effortlessly produces course after course of perfectly cooked food. Jock calls her the best cook in France and from a foodie of his calibre, this is no small compliment.

When I finally do decide I need a telephone connection, it's Lucienne who organises the entire complicated rigmarole for me, in just a few minutes. She also kindly offers to speak simple French conversation with me if I pop in for a cup of coffee on my way through Pomarède, but somehow I never seem to quite find the time. I wonder to myself if I am avoiding the issue, or if I am simply overcome with embarrassment at my ineptitude. As a person accustomed to being in control of things, floundering over the most simple conversation is quite galling. I would like at least to be able to manage some simple sentences before inflicting my stumbling mispronunciations on someone as charming and sophisticated as Lucienne. I also feel it's ill-mannered of me not being able to speak the language of a country that I adore living in. So when people like Philippe tease me from time to time for my verbal ignorance, I feel truly chastened. Mind you, there are plenty of other non-French speakers living here in the Lot full time who have not attempted to speak much French at all, but I certainly don't want to be like them. I realise I lack a natural facility with languages and know it will be a long, hard struggle.

17

I BUY A PHONE CARD TO use in the public telephone booth, but calls to Australia devour 100 ff ($25) in no time at all. Then I notice that the phone box has a number, and I decide to try an experiment with David. I give him the number so he can call me back. It feels odd standing in a glass box waiting for the phone to ring. But it works perfectly and we are finally in regular communication. I give the number of my corner phone box to my children and the routine is that on Sunday morning (Sunday evening in Australia) I use my phone card to let them know I am in the phone box. For the first time we have long chats, and I feel so much more at ease knowing that everything is okay at home. I describe my view of the world from the phone box.

'I can see a round stone tower with blue shutters. The streets are cobbled and very narrow and everyone has to stand against the wall when a car goes past. There's an antique fair this weekend and the place is packed with stalls and buyers. Here comes an old man with a black beret, carrying a bread stick under his arm, just like in the movies. Here comes one of the cats I'm feeding—it's started yowling because it's recognised me through the glass.'

The children are called to the phone to say hello to Mutie, but Eamonn still simply refuses to cooperate. According to Miriam he goes very quiet when the subject of his errant grandmother in France is discussed, and has even told her, 'I don't want to talk about it'. He must be feeling really miffed and is punishing me for abandoning him. It works. I feel terrible.

In late July, Aaron and a heavily pregnant Lorna move into our house in the Blue Mountains with Hamish, giving up their rental property. David has now gone to Queensland for at least three months of solid filming, and there are so many animals to look after that leaving the house empty is out of the question, even though it's quite stressful for Lorna to move so close to when her baby is due. I call on Sunday morning and I feel happy to hear her voice sounding settled and relaxed at last. I ask to speak to Hamish and he comes on line. Late afternoon is a noto-riously bad time for three-year-olds and I should have expected some trouble.

'Where ARE you, Mutie?' he asks with a tremble in his voice.

'In France, darling, a long way away.'

'I want you, Mutie, I want you now.' His voice is thick with tiredness.

'I'll be home in a few months, darling. At Christmas. Do you remember I told you that I will be home at Christmas?'

'But I want you back NOW, Mutie, I want you NOW,' he wails, and starts to sob. Then shriek. In the background I can hear Aaron getting involved, talking calmly to Hamish and taking him out of the room. He sounds as though he is throwing a proper wobbly, and when Lorna comes on line she's crying. So am I, standing in a phone box, tears cascading down my cheeks. It's pathetic.

Generally, however, the calls home on Sundays are a great success and everyone feels better for a routine chat. I try not to call when the children are at their low, late afternoon ebb. Or during meal or bath times, which are always chaotic.

My most heartfelt wrench living in France is the sudden lack of regular communication with my daughter Miriam, with whom I am particularly close. I have grown accustomed to lengthy gaps in my relationship with David, because of him being away so often filming, but even when Miriam was at university in Canberra she was only three hours away. Now not speaking to her for literally weeks at a time feels weird. Sending off the odd postcard doesn't feel like making a real connection at all, and the idea of writing and posting letters is clunky and slow when you are accustomed to the efficiency of electronic communications. Miriam's computer has no email connection, so she goes over to our house and uses mine whenever she can escape from her three small boys, sending me long emails which I pick up the next day at Jock's. They are generally packed with news and information, but also tinged with a certain poignancy.

'If I've ever taken you for granted, Mum, and I hope I never have, I certainly never will again,' she writes, in relation to the business of managing three boisterous sons with a husband away long hours commuting to his job in the city, and a reckless mother who has abandoned her to the task.

I don't feel even slightly guilty at her words, knowing that she supports the notion of my escape from responsibility whole-heartedly, but I do miss her and the little boys badly, and feel a constant longing for the warmth I always feel in their company. This bond that we have is a joy: I know that such relationships are by no means automatic. More than a few of my middle-aged female friends have deeply troubled relationships with their mothers; unresolved problems that may date back to childhood, but probably manifested themselves in their teenage years. Over time these adult female friends have voiced their amazement that I should get along so well with my own mother. That I should actually enjoy having her living under the same roof as me for several decades.

I have often tried to fathom why these mother and daughter relationships have failed so badly, and it seems that several factors come into play. The question of control is a major issue for many mothers who try to squash the natural development of their teenage daughters as they emerge into womanhood. If the daughter has a strong or rebellious personality then conflict is inevitable as the power struggle continues—and it can do so for decades unless an effort is made to resolve it. Then there's that strange form of jealousy that sometimes manifests itself when the daughter begins to blossom in her teens. It seems quite amazing to me that a mother could resent or feel threatened by her daughter's beauty and sexuality. It's something to celebrate rather than to resent. The issue of sibling rivalry is also often discussed at length by disaffected daughters. They believe that their mother's love was stolen by another member of the family, usually a brother, 'The apple of his mother's eye'. How a mother could favour one child over another is difficult to comprehend, but I know it must be true. Otherwise why would all these women believe it with such conviction? For one close friend of mine this alienation of love so affected her life that she postponed having a child for nearly two decades. Then when she finally decided in her late thirties to take the plunge, she spent her entire pregnancy worrying that it might be a girl. She obviously dreaded a mother–daughter relationship that may have eventually turned out like her own. Luckily, I suppose, she had a beautiful son.

Having a good relationship with Miriam was never hard because she was always so easygoing. A self-sufficient, rather serious and thoughtful child who loved school and even seemed to quite enjoy being the only girl in a family of three noisy boys. Naturally she went through some rocky patches in her teens, but nothing more than the usual angst experienced by any bright, sensitive young woman establishing her place in the world. Of course my tendency to avoid being a confrontational parent undoubtedly made those teenage years less troublesome, especially as I adopted a fairly passive stance to her more minor rebellions such as choice of clothing, hair colouring or body piercings. My attitude has always been that these issues are fairly superficial and not worth fighting about. Better to save arguments for more important teenage problems, such as drug-taking and unprotected sex. In her mid teens Miriam went through a gothic phase, draped in black rags and with alarming pillarbox red hair, but she didn't show any inclination to get mixed up with boys until she was seventeen and had passed that dangerous hormonal phase that drives parents of younger teenage daughters crazy. She excelled in her final school exams and emerged in her university years as a level-headed and eminently likeable young woman.

David and I were rather surprised when Miriam launched herself into motherhood at such an early age, but when I thought about it I realised she was only following the pattern that I had set myself. Our real closeness as mother and adult daughter developed quickly around the births of her three children and through the sudden death of my mother, her grandmother. There is nothing like birth and death to ground a relationship, and ours certainly did just that during a period of five action-packed years. Miriam's first baby was born in the bedroom of the small flat she shared with fellow uni student Rick, who later became her husband. In attendance at the birth were me, Rick, and Miriam's youngest brother Ethan, who was then fourteen. The midwife had a migraine headache and spent quite a bit of the labour in the next room, lying in the dark. When it came time for Miriam to start bearing down she reappeared, crowned the head, then allowed me to catch my first grandson and hand him to my daughter. It was a moment of such intimacy and love that everything before and since has slightly paled.

My mother died suddenly while Miriam was pregnant with her second child. Sensing my fragility, Miriam was constantly at my side, especially during those few surrealistic days between the death and the gathering of the clan for the send-off. The hardest thing we have ever done together was to prepare Mum's body on the morning of the funeral. Neither of us had ever seen a dead person before, but we wanted to be the ones to brush her tangle of grey hair into place and perhaps apply a little makeup in case we felt the mood was right for a viewing of the body by our assembled family and friends later that morning. We had an early morning cup of tea with Mum's coffin sitting on the kitchen table. The funeral director had given detailed directions on how to unscrew and open the lid, which we did with more than a little trepidation. When we saw Mum lying there, so still, we looked up at each other with relief.

'It isn't her,' Miriam said. 'It's her body, but Grandma isn't there.'

What she said was exactly the truth. Yes, my mother's face in rest was recognisable, but her spirit had entirely gone. There was nothing there, just a shell. But we gently combed her hair then massaged a little makeup into her cold, tight skin. To my horror one of her eyes suddenly popped open, and I gingerly pulled the eyelid back to cover it, hoping it wouldn't open again to wink at everyone if we did decide to lift the lid. It was a moment I probably would have found almost impossible to share with David, or with one of my sons. But somehow with Miriam and I working together, tending a loved one in death as so many women have before us, it felt just right.

A few months later Miriam gave birth to her second son, Sam, this time in a little old cottage she and Rick had recently bought in Katoomba. Every man and his dog was at that birth, and I'll always remember David sitting in my mother's old rocking chair, which I had since passed on to Miriam, and sleeping through the most torrid and noisy part of the labour. Two years later a third son, Theo, was also born at her home, by which time I had amassed the most wonderful collection of photographs and even videos of these intense family occasions. Theo was born late one Saturday afternoon and Miriam and Rick decided, despite his newness, to bring him and his brothers to our house for our ritual Sunday lunch. I have a photograph of David asleep in his big old wingback chair, snoozing after lunch with his less-than-day-old grandson tucked in the crook of his arm. To be included in the births of your grandchildren is a privilege, perhaps not one that every grandparent would relish, but one that I wouldn't have missed out on for all the world.

18

APART FROM THE ANTIQUES and book fairs there are regular village fêtes which are also a major feature of the summer months. Each town and village has a set weekend for their festivities, so as not to clash with each other, and the event usually involves two days of celebrations with colourful circus-style children's rides trucked in and set up in the town square. The Saturday evening event, called a 'repas', is a feast of traditional foods prepared by the women and served on long wooden trestle tables under the moonlight. There are lively bands, light shows, dancing and fireworks, and all the village people and farming families come together in a celebration of the season. Visitors and holidaymakers are always welcome, and in St Caprais Jock is always greatly admired for his ability to fill a table with friends, and therefore boost the success of the event. This year's St Caprais fête is held over the first weekend in July, and the weather is perfect—if it rains the villagers have to put up a marquee, which spoils the ambience of dining outdoors in the ancient square.

The St Caprais fête has the reputation of being one of the liveliest in the region. During this period I am visited by two Australian backpackers—Jenny, the daughter of a dear friend from the Blue Mountains who died several years ago, and her friend Anthea from university days. They are two-thirds of the way through a six-month, ten-country tour of Europe and are badly in need of a break from youth hostels and railway journeys. Jock, generous as ever, offers them a room and two comfortable beds, and they love the region so much they decide to explore Toulouse then return to St Caprais for the fête.

More than thirty friends gather at Jock's for a drink before-hand, and the mood is relaxed and happy. There are dozens of children, both French and English-speaking, playing in the square, where a bar tent provides draught beer, aperitifs and wine to augment the jugs of quaffing red that are served as part of the 100 ff menu. It is nine o'clock by the time we are seated at the long tables, with the setting sun glowing on the creamy stone facades of the tall buildings that surround the square. There is a disco playing in the background—fortunately not loud enough to swamp the convivial conversation—and a woman singer who can certainly belt out a tune. We start with traditional tourin blanchi (white soup) with plenty of garlic and bread in the broth, followed by a rough pâté du porc that has the most intense flavour. The meat is being barbecued over an open fire and the fragrance is mouthwatering; the lamb cutlets will be served with huge bowls of steaming white beans in rich sauce. During all this the wine is flowing and the village children are throwing more and more lengths of crusty bread onto the table to mop up all the wonderful sauces and juices. Crisp green salad follows, with more bread and platters of cheese including the famous Cantal and some wonderful soft goat cheeses. More wine and then the dancing starts, with the music now blaring and lights flashing against the backdrop of mediaeval buildings. I find myself linking arms with farmers and their wives, leaping around the square with total joy and abandon, then dashing back to the table for apple tart and just a touch more red wine. Children are dancing with their grandparents, teenagers are snogging in the corners and the bar tent is doing a roaring trade. It's well after 2 am by the time I slink back to Jock's to collapse, having decided that driving back to Villefranche isn't such a crash-hot idea. The music continues for quite some time and I imagine there will be some monumental hangovers around tomorrow, not just mine.

Next day the restaurant across the road is having a Sunday lunch and somehow Jock and I scrape ourselves together to start eating and drinking again by midday. The backpacking girls are looking worn but quickly rally at the thought of more fine food. They are both so skinny I wonder where they are putting it all. Lunch is naturally another six-course extravaganza and we are barely able to walk when the time comes to leave in the late afternoon. Kind friends give me a lift home and I sleep comfortably in a dead coma for twelve hours. Sadly, I miss the last evening of the fête, which is apparently an absolute hoot. An all-female dancing group called Johnny and the Boys perform to loud head banging music in the square, dashing into a grotty caravan to change outfits between brackets. Close to midnight there are fireworks against the church wall, and miraculously everyone manages to recover by Monday morning. The square has been cleaned and looks pristine, the tractors are back in the fields and the rhythm of life returns to normal.

There are two village feasts in Loubejac, the first being a moules et frites night early in the season which is my introduction to these communal outdoor parties. On this occasion a massive bonfire is set ablaze in the field beside the church, and following an ancient custom, we hold hands in a huge ring, dancing round and round the fire wildly in a stumbling circle to the clapping of hands from the assembled throng; in some of the villages the young men jump over the embers when the fire dies down. The main Loubejac repas, held in August, is a méchoui, or spit roasted lamb for the main course, which is enormously popular. Indeed, we are lucky to have bought seats early in the evening because by 9 pm there is a queue 100 metres long and in the end dozens of groups are turned away disappointed. This fête is quite stylish and more sophisticated than most, with a timber dance floor set up inside a marquee, disco lights and a snappy band.

After the wonderful meal I enjoy a few spins around the dance floor with Roger, a man whom Jock regards as his best ally here in France. Roger is certainly one of the more eccentric English imports, dashing and lovable in a curious, oldfashioned way. A romantic figure and somewhat solitary, Roger is a talented artist in his early fifties who has been living in France on and off for thirty years. He's been married and divorced but now lives back in Brighton during the winter with his ex-wife who in turn comes to stay for a month or so in France during the summer. They are an interesting couple, who spend more than half of every year living apart, perhaps because they have established themselves as individuals. Every spring Roger abandons Brighton and rushes back to his small stone house in Loubejac, which has a well-tended garden and panoramic views down to fields and woodland copses. In many ways Roger sees himself as a French peasant in the traditional sense—living off his wits and the land rather than cold, hard cash: he cultivates an excellent vegetable and fruit garden and knows exactly where to gather nuts, fruits and wild mushrooms in the woods. He bottles and preserves fruit during gluts and has a good eye for wine, which he buys bulk, bottles himself then puts down for several years to mature. As he's also a great cook, a meal at Roger's place is always an event, but he seldom joins us in our restaurant outings or village fêtes, except for his own local Loubejac repas. Way back, he decided that long lunches were not a great idea for one's health or waistline, and he calls Jock, with his penchant for whiling away so many hours at the table, 'Sir Lunchalot'.

Roger speaks excellent regional French, having been among the first wave of English to descend upon this part of the world, and is a mine of information about the local customs and way of life. He mourns the passing of the small, farm-based vineyards around Loubejac, which provided so much community spirit during harvesting times when neighbours rallied to get the grapes in on time. What vines remain in the area are now mechanically harvested. Each farm once produced its own wine, but these days it's considered too labour intensive, especially as the mass-produced wines are so cheap. Roger also regrets the introduction of the huge hay-baling machines which mean that locals no longer rush to each other's fields in the late afternoon to help gather the small bales on the back of a cart to be put under cover lest rain falls during the night. It was this sense of helpfulness that made Roger feel bonded to his neighbours, and certainly here at the Loubejac repas Roger is regarded very much as a local, not just a foreign fly-by-nighter.

Following his example, I try some restraint, limiting myself to just a few glasses of the rich and heavy local red wine, though I still decide that it's more sensible to drive back to Villefranche through the woods rather than down the main road. I can see no moon or stars and the woods late at night are black as pitch. As I round one sharp corner my headlights catch sight of a huge barn owl sitting in the middle of the road. It turns and gives me a cold stare before flying off into the dark.

The Pomarède fête is also on a larger scale than the one at St Caprais. I join a mixed crowd that gathers for pre-dinner drinks on Lucienne's leafy terrace, then wanders to the square as the sun is going down. It's a handsome square indeed, fronting the church which is in the midst of some major restoration work. There are lots of children's rides and circus-style sideshows, the obligatory bar tent and plenty of loud music. This time the village organisers have opted for the more traditional piano accordion group, which provides the style of music that the older couples enjoy dancing to. As the evening progresses and the various courses are laid along the tables, the couples swirl around the square, husbands holding their wives tightly against them as they spin and perform some fancy footwork. It's a terrific floor show but I don't feel confident enough of my formal dancing skills to join in. The children rush around the sideshows, shrieking with delight as they return to the tables clutching cheap plastic prizes won at the stalls. I wonder where the teenagers who served our meal have disappeared to. The music somehow isn't quite their speed, and I later see them in a huddle drinking, smoking and talking intimately.

In Frayssinet there is a fête de la bière (beer festival) at the end of July, organised by the local football club. Instead of the usual black beret, these club members wear bright yellow ones which make them look like a bunch of demented bumble bees as they set up the beer tents and trestle tables. The meal is choucroute and sausages, and the entertainment is to be provided by a country music group called Chicken Gerry and his Hot Potatoes. Who could resist? Another gorgeous twilight and the square behind the school is slow to fill so we end up drinking several beers while waiting for things to get underway. When it does finally arrive the choucroute is remarkable—a plate piled high with steaming spicy cabbage covered with about five different types of sausage and salted pork. There are various mustards and chunks of crispy bread—the crust of the bread here is so crunchy that you can easily cut your gums or tongue when eating. Choucroute is another dish that has its origins in Germany, but has long been adopted as a hearty dish, although in the French version the cabbage is much sweeter—and because it is still high summer, and very hot indeed, we feel a need to wash it down with more and more ice cold beer.

It's quite late when Chicken Gerry takes to the stage and starts to play, but the peculiar brand of French-style Irish country music, featuring electric fiddle and guitar, is terrific. Before long half our table is dancing a wild jig, with the beer and cabbage swirling around inside. After an hour or so of this frenetic bopping my stomach feels fit to explode its deadly contents and for once I am defeated, making my way home well before midnight.

One of the most popular summer activities is the circus, which spends four months travelling through the southwest, setting up in a new village square every second day. There are two or three troupes, and the one that visits our region is ominously called 'Albatross Circus', although it has a fine wagon train of modern trailers and caravans. The big top is impressive too, and also quite new, giving the appearance of an extremely slick and professional outfit. They arrive in Villefranche early one Sunday morning and tie their animals up in the triangle of grass that marks the entrance to the village. There are two midget horses, several goats, a donkey, a dog and a llama. The posters have been up for several days, advertising a starting time of 9 pm, which seems to me rather late to be taking small children to the circus. The tent goes up in the small square outside the post office, along with a drink and food caravan and a ticket booth. I saunter along at 8.30 and feel alarmed to see few people and little activity. A storm is threatening and I am concerned that it's going to be a flop. Eventually, at about 9.15, dozens of families with children of all ages start to arrive, and the circus members eventually begin selling tickets. It's close to ten o'clock by the time the show gets underway. The Hollywood-style circus music blasts from several loudspeakers and the performers enter the ring.

There are two men, a youngish woman and two children—a boy about fourteen and I presume his young sister who looks about nine. She is blonde, very pretty and dressed in colourful leotards. One of the small horses, with feather plumes attached to its head, opens the show. The taller of the men, in clown costume, stands in the centre of the ring and the horse, attached to a long rope, canters around the ring about twenty times. The horse prances into the centre and lifts one of his front hooves into the air, receiving wild applause. He repeats this sequence three or four times, each time ending with the cute hoof-in-air finale. More applause. A large drum is brought into the ring and the small horse somewhat reluctantly places his two front hooves on the top of the drum. He then lifts one hoof into the air and the crowd goes wild.

Next the teenage boy performs some unsteady juggling tricks and every time he drops a ring or baton his little sister runs into the spotlight and throws her arms in the air for an audience reaction. They clap enthusiastically. The little girl then does a few acrobatic flips and handstands, the last few from the top of two tables. Act four is the clown and the young woman in a small mime act that involves him stuffing various objects down his pants; it's quite amusing, and the children appreciate the humour. The first half culminates in an act with a goat performing exactly the same routine as the small horse. The only difference is that, being a goat, he is capable of standing on a stack of three barrels before lifting his front hoof for the grand finale.

During interval the performers staff the drinks tent, selling beer, Pepsi and popcorn. The little girl works hard flogging lucky dips to every family with a child—she manages to offload at least fifty parcels. She then comes around with a hat held out for donations. Given that the door price was quite high and that most families have also had to shell out for drinks, popcorn and lucky dips, I fear for many it will be quite an expensive night out.

The second half differs little from the first, except that the shorter man, in a leotard and white singlet, performs a balancing act on a plank of wood and a cylinder placed on a table, about one metre from the ground. It is quite a simple routine, but he is playing it for all it's worth, jumping off every few minutes and inviting applause. Halfway through a stray dog enters the tent and wanders into the centre of the ring, sitting directly beneath the table where the balancing man is performing. He then proceeds to lick his testicles enthusiastically, which sends the crowd wild. The performer naturally assumes the reaction is in appreciation of his act, and beams with delight.

The last act is the llama, which goes through exactly the same routine previously performed by the small horse and the goat. Round and round he dashes, then into the centre and up with the hoof. The music ends and the audience straggles out just as the storm starts. The whole proceedings, including the interval, have taken just under an hour and by lunchtime the next day the big top and wagon train have vanished. As if they were never there at all.

19

THERE ARE SOME THINGS in life that are impossible to escape, and for me gardening is one of them. I was quite looking forward to a break from the responsibility and hard slog of maintaining a large garden, but so many of my new friends have gardens that I can't help but get a little enthusiastic and involved. The plants used in the average landscape are basically the same, with the exception of a dearth of Australian native species, but the techniques are a little different. In the local nurseries I see that old-fashioned roses are popular over here again, just as they are back home, and by the wide range on sale it's clear that people also love to grow herbs for cooking and productive fruiting trees and shrubs. I am told that the winters in the southwest are much harsher than those at home, and I know the summers—as I have experienced them first-hand—are very hot and dry. There is a great emphasis on summer colour, with gaily flowering begonias, pelargoniums and petunias in pots and tubs outside virtually every front door. Lots of energy is also invested in growing vegetables. It looks like a lot of fun.

When I first start chatting about gardens to the French, I realise they automatically presume I am talking about a potager, or vegetable patch. The average garden surrounding a house is seldom more than trees and lawn, and those trees are usually productive rather than ornamental. Walnut, fig and apples are all popular garden specimens because they look pretty and provide a yield for harvesting at some stage of the year. The main effort of gardening is directed into growing good things to eat, and everywhere I walk or drive I spot these potagers, small patches of earth supporting magnificent displays of tomatoes, salad vegetables, climbing beans, zucchinis and spring onions. Even in the larger towns there are potager gardens squeezed into odd sunny corners in the most unlikely places, and there are also allotments on the outskirts for people who live in apartments or townhouses. This preference for growing plants that are useful rather than decorative is surely a hangover from the days when people struggled to find food for the pot all year round. These days it looks like a land of plenty, but in times gone by the poorer farmers and woodcutters of the region did not have access to the wild game that is now so abundant, and therefore they had to ensure a steady supply of cultivated food. Growing food became a way of life, and it has remained the same ever since.

The gardens established by newcomers—the English in particular—always stand apart. The English have much more interest in developing wide beds and borders for planting collections of flowering ornamentals, and when you see gardens in this style dotted around the countryside, you know that they have not been created by farming families. Most of Jock's friends can't resist creating these English-style ornamental gardens, although they usually also try and incorporate a small potager or at the very least a herb garden for the summer months.

When the urge strikes me to potter in a garden I start by attacking Jock's small courtyard, which is a shambles. Overgrown with weeds, the soil is impenetrable when I try and use a spade to dig over the area where he has in previous seasons grown summer vegetables. He doesn't ask for my assistance, but it's obvious he needs more than a little help knocking it into shape, and it's the least I can do to repay his ongoing kindness. Before I arrived, he had planted a few tomatoes against the stone walls, but they are struggling now because of the weed competition. The main weed is a most unpleasant stinging nettle which I quickly discover brings me out in a red, angry rash. I will need gloves and long pants and plenty of patience.

I have a bit of an obsession about compost and I can't abide wasting kitchen vegetable scraps by throwing them out with the rubbish. Jock does a fair bit of cooking and there are always plenty of peelings, so I establish a small compost heap in one corner, using the discarded weeds as a base. I first chop them up into small sections with the sharp end of the spade, then layer them with some manure that I scrounge from the roadside nearby. It feels so good being in an area where the essential ingredients of composting are so readily available. Prunings and weeds, manure and straw are all it takes to make a rich mound of fertile humus, and I take pleasure in watering the fresh heap lightly to start the decomposing process.

The ground is totally unyielding, so eventually I resort to using a crowbar to clear the area of weeds and hundreds of irritating small stones. Over a period of twenty years in my own garden, I have transformed a large sunny area into a lush vegetable patch by consistently layering mulches and composts on top of the fragile, sandy surface. These days I can slide a spade into the soil and it's like cutting butter, so I find it frustrating to be working on ground that is so tough and unwelcoming. I stockpile the stones and later use them to create a small neat edging between the garden bed and the lawn. Jock and I trundle off to the Prayssac market to buy seedlings to fill the space when it's finally cleared and level and weed free. Unlike Australian nurseries, where seedlings are produced commercially en masse and sold in small plastic punnets that hold ten or twelve young plants, the seedlings here are on display in large wooden trays so they can be separated and bought as required. This is a great way of doing things, because you can buy just a few of each vegetable variety at a time, and plant them successively over the season. I can plant a few zucchinis now, and in four weeks another two or three so that Jock can be harvesting well into autumn and winter. The range is a bit limited, reflecting the type of vegetables that are available in the market. Apart from several young zucchini plants, we buy English spinach, dwarf beans, and a variety of herbs including broad leaf parsley and chives. Jan, who has been propagating all sorts of wonderful flowering annuals and herbs in Claude's pretty glasshouse, donates a good selection to our 'Tarting up Jock's garden' cause. On the way back from Prayssac we stop off at the local nursery to buy a few bags of manure, then pause for a long lunch at Madame Murat's on the way home. Needless to say I don't feel much like gardening on this particular afternoon.

Being so small, Jock's garden is transformed in no time at all, and he is delighted with the results. He tells all our friends he is doing me a big favour, allowing me to garden in his courtyard.

'She's obviously missing her garden. It's the very least I can do to let her use mine.'

The days are long and hot and the garden flourishes. The soil that I had cursed when digging over the patch is obviously highly fertile, and the vegetables grow at such a rate that keeping up with the harvest almost becomes a chore. The zucchinis in particular are rampant, and Jock makes pot after pot of zucchini soup, to the point where we start to get sick of eating it. Some of the zucchinis grow to the size of marrows, and he is always trying to foist them onto friends and neighbours. Half the time he doesn't make it down the back steps to check on the progress of the plants, and I find myself harvesting tomatoes and beans that have been left too long on the vine. Without constant attention the garden gradually becomes overgrown again, and I realise that I will need to tend it weekly if it is to remain under control. Perhaps it should have been paved over and turned into an outdoor dining room.

I also spend a happy afternoon in the garden of Jock's English actress friend Pam. Twice widowed, Pam is now living in a new house that has been cleverly recreated in the old style, overlooking the ancient hillside township of Puy-l'Evêque. Pam was well over sixty when she decided to live full time in France and she has, unlike certain retirees, made a concerted effort to study the language and culture. She zips off to various formal language and conversation classes and spends a lot of time speaking French with Lucienne who encourages her tremendously. Meeting Pam and seeing that it is possible for an older brain to absorb all the things there are to learn gives me great hope that I too will eventually get the hang of speaking the language. I had almost reached a point of thinking my mind was too overloaded and addled for it, but Pam, quite a bit older than I am, proves you can assimilate on many levels. She joins in all the summer activities—antique sales and village meals—but also loves to spend time alone in her garden where she encourages birds by the hundreds to feel at home. Having been a professional actress in her younger days, Pam still has an air about her that is utterly disarming. Jock calls her a 'lady, in the nicest sense of the word'. Now over seventy, Pam isn't coy about her age, but she refuses to reveal it because of the prejudice sometimes directed against older women. She believes, and she's probably right, that if people knew her age they would think about her quite differently. I wonder if when I am in my seventies I will encounter the same sort of attitudes.

Pam asks me for some help in constructing a raised bed in an area where plants have been failing to thrive. Her garden is built on a difficult sloping site, again with masses of rocks and stones right through the soil, making it extremely tricky to cultivate. The small amount of soil she has imported needs constantly to be retained or it simply washes away every time it rains. There are plenty of good chunky rocks for building up the edges of a raised bed and once again we head off to the local nursery to pick up some extra soil-building organic matter and some plants to fill up the newly created space. It's fun looking at all the different products and plants available in another country, but I realise that I would be stumped trying to buy a bag of potting mix or special purpose fertiliser because the labelling is so hard to interpret. Maybe I should start my language-building skills by concentrating on learning how to translate bagged gardening products.

Back at Pam's, we nestle the new roses and annuals into place and water them in. I am amazed at how much she has achieved single-handedly on such a difficult site, and can only encourage her to keep on with it. My philosophy with gardens that involve a lot of physical exertion is to tackle just a small area at a time. If you start looking at the garden as a whole entity you can be quite daunted; many people are defeated before they even begin. But if you just chip away at a small square at a time you can, over several months or years, achieve a tremendous amount. The fact that so many hundreds of native birds visit Pam's pretty garden on a daily basis, for food and water and nectar from the plants, is a testament to her success against the gardening odds.

One of the loveliest gardens I come to know belongs to Danny, a softly-spoken man who has restored a classic Quercy farmhouse, with a pigeonnier tower and spacious barn, into a holiday retreat which he rents out every summer. Danny's partner Sue died unexpectedly of a cerebral aneurysm barely six months before I arrived on the scene, and he is still very much in a state of shock and grief when I meet him. He's camping in the barn from June until September while the main house is occupied by holidaymakers. Born in France, one of six children, he was sent to live in England with an aunt and uncle at the age of six after the death of his mother. His siblings remained with his father in France, but he and his brother who were reared in England lost their native language. It's not surprising, however, that he should end up living in the beautiful country of his birth, and he is much adored within the expatriate community as well as by his farming neighbours. Everyone tells me how well-loved Sue also was. She is affectionately described as a 'real gardener', because that was her particular passion. Over the years, while Danny worked away on the house restoration, Sue created the beautiful garden that made the entire property so appealing.

Danny shows me dozens of photographs of Sue taken in the last couple of years of her life. Her open sunny face beams out with such vivacity that I feel somehow as though I know her. Like me she was born in 1950, and would have celebrated her fiftieth birthday this year, here in their beautiful farmhouse, with Danny and all their friends around her. Now she has suddenly vanished, leaving Danny and the garden to survive alone. Naturally it's become overgrown during the summer and there's a real risk that it will get totally out of control. Having worked briefly in Jock and Pam's stony yards I can appreciate just how much back-breaking work Sue must have put into the vast areas around the old house and barn, chiselling richly planted garden beds from the harsh soil and introducing a diverse range of species, from old-fashioned roses to alpines. I can tell that she was quite a plantswoman and feel a tremendous sense of sadness that she is no longer around to revel in the abundance of her handywork. Many of the plants she has used are the same as those in my Leura garden, so luckily I am familiar with their habits and foibles. As autumn comes in, many of the shrubs and perennials desperately need cutting back, and I offer to spend a few days in the garden to knock it into shape.

My time in Danny's garden coincides with his repairs to the barn roof that was blown down in a violent January storm. This damage to the property all happened about the same time as Sue's death, and restoring the barn to its former glory has been a long, heartbreaking haul for him. He is now at the stage of replacing the last rows of roof tiles, which involves tying a long safety rope to himself and clambering over the roof framework which is at least twenty metres from ground level. It's alarming, and I am just pleased that I can be around working in the garden to keep an eye on him—otherwise, if he had a fall he would have to wait until a neighbour came looking for him. Not a very satisfactory thought.

In glorious weather, I spend three or four days clipping, pruning and deadheading Sue's precious plants. All the while I am working away I carry on an imaginary conversation with her, in my mind describing for her benefit just how well it's all coming together. The garden sweeps around three sides of the property, framing a large in-ground swimming pool and set against a backdrop of sunny open fields. There are large areas of lawn edged with curved beds that have been crammed with clumps of iris, fragrant lavender and shrubby roses. Against the creamy stone walls Sue has planted climbing roses and allowed them to wander rampantly; many need pruning back and tidying up if they are to continue flowering prolifically. There are small garden beds around the swimming pool, planted with pelargoniums, variegated oregano and various perennials tough enough to survive the heat in this area, which is magnified by the paving around the pool. There's a deep pond alive with chirping frogs, and nearby huge clumps of artichokes that are in full flower during the summer. Their dramatic purple-blue blooms work brilliantly with the traditional blue of the painted timber house shutters, and I wonder if Sue planned this association deliberately. If she didn't, it is definitely a very happy accident.

I am delighted to find that Sue had a huge composting system, and I add all my prunings to the latest heap. I also take some cuttings of various shrubs and perennials, which I get going in a small bed that she had set aside for propagation.

While working away I wonder how my own garden at home is

surviving without me for such a long time. During winter it won't prove a problem, but when spring and summer arrive I know too well that the same sorts of problems that I am tackling here will also be happening at home. Even though I have mulched deeply through most of the beds, I know that various perennial weeds will not be daunted by this tactic. Buttercups, in particular, have a tendency to go mad despite all attempts to control them and I fully expect to arrive back at Christmas and find a jungle in all directions.

But for now I can concentrate on helping Sue's garden through another season, and hoping that in time it will settle into a pattern that doesn't require too much maintenance. Just as every garden reflects the gardener's individual style and personality, Sue's design shows her love of informality. The generous sweeping flower beds have curved edges and are overflowing with her most treasured plants. However it's not a garden that will simply look after itself—it was obviously her intention to go on working in the garden for many years to come. True gardeners never 'finish' their work. It's an ongoing process of change and renewal as plants mature and as the gardener's tastes, knowledge and interests change. So Sue's garden is in a holding pattern, with just a little tender care from me until another gardener comes along to claim it.

20

IF ANYONE WAS TO SUGGEST six months ago that I would be tucking into a warm salad of duck's gizzards and loving every mouthful I'd have laughed. Or gagged. Offal of any description has never been my favourite fare. In this part of France fatty ducks and geese are one of the main specialities, and the thrifty resourceful farmers waste no part of the animal—fat, flesh, gizzards and even skin are all put to good use. Foie gras, the rich liver of force-fed geese, is produced here by the thousands of kilos; and other specialities include cassoulet and gésiers, or sautéed duck's innards. They are wonderfully succulent served warm on a bed of lettuce with walnuts and a light dressing of walnut oil and vinegar.

There's a well-publicised rumour around these parts that goose and duck fat is actually GOOD fat. Some pundits even claim that it has cholesterol-lowering properties and the proof offered is that people of this region have the lowest cholesterol levels in France, certainly much lower than in those provinces where cream and butter are the specialities. Whether it's the combination of the fatty ducks and geese washed down with gallons of red wine that has health-giving benefits, or whether the whole promotional campaign is designed to encourage guilt-free consumption, I still have no doubt that eating lots of our web-footed friends is fattening. I am living proof of this.

The local supermarket shelves are groaning with tins of confit du canard and succulent cuts of duck meat unheard of outside France, including maigret, a breast fillet that is seared on a hotplate then cooked lightly so that it is pink or red inside, like the rarest fillet of steak. It is often barbecued with equally mouth-watering results. It is also possible to buy filleted breasts of dinde (turkey) which also respond well to light cooking and are more flavoursome than plain chicken breasts.

Confit du canard is portions of duck meat—usually leg and thigh—preserved in duck fat, and it is sold either tinned or fresh from a good quality charcuterie, the open marketplace and even the supermarket. The fat is scraped away gently so as not to damage the crinkly skin, then the confit is heated in a frying pan, with the main side turned pan downwards at the end to make the skin crispy. It can also be grilled just before serving to produce the same crunchy effect. This last-minute grilling is also given to the other local speciality, cassoulet. Nothing could be more French than a cassoulet made with love—white haricot beans, confit of duck or goose, mutton, salt pork, garlic sausage, tomatoes, and breadcrumbs to thicken the sauce and become crisp and toasty when the dish is grilled before serving. Heaven.

Another warm and fuzzy rumour going around suggests that ducks and geese actually enjoy being force-fed. That they line up for their turn at having a pipe inserted into their gullet so that several cups of corn can be pumped in via a noisy machine. Well of course they line up, otherwise they'd starve to death or be chased around and force-fed regardless. But the way in which they fall to the ground and are unable to move for a while after being crammed full with grain suggests they are not having the time of their lives. After a few weeks of this, when their livers are practically exploding, they are given the final curtain. It's not a duck or goose paradise here, that's for sure.

The specialities of Périgord and Quercy are duck and goose, pork in all its various forms, walnuts and walnut oil, mushrooms including the sought after cepes and giroles, precious truffles and a dark red wine that is produced extensively around Cahors. Also included in the traditional diet are apples and pears that grow on gnarled old trees all around the country lanes; succulent prunes from the southern city of Agen which are often cooked with pork and wine; chestnuts that cover the floor of the woodlands in autumn; a soft and fragrant goat cheese called cabecou as well as a blue known as Bleu des Casses which is similar in taste and texture to Roquefort; flavourful fresh strawberries in the spring and summer; and vegetables and fruit including small but brilliant orange-fleshed melons and rich pumpkins at the end of the season. The open markets reflect the availability of produce and although, like any modern part of the world, you can visit the supermarket and buy bananas or pineapples most of the year round, the most popular cuisine is really based upon what is grown or raised locally.

In the autumn the chasse or hunting season gets underway, and white vans parked along the sides of all the roads combined with the sound of dogs barking and the ring of gunshot all weekend mean that wild boar and venison will soon be available. These can be bought at the marketplace but they are also served up at traditional chasse dinners or fêtes where the menu has nothing but wild foods. The idea of eating a sumptuous banquet from foods hunted or gathered in the woodlands is very appealing, although I will not be around in February when these fêtes are generally held. People assure me it's hard to get up from the table after the three- or four-hour-long eating 'ordeal'.

One of the features of the cuisine is the use of goose fat for sautéeing and frying. Fat from confit is always reserved and used for sautéeing crisp potatoes that are served as an accompaniment to the melting duck. Snowy white goose fat is also sold in glass jars in the supermarket for all manner of frying—the secret is not just the flavour it imparts to the food but the fact that it cooks hotter than most oils, and therefore the results are wonderfully crisp. I still don't believe, however, that frying batches of potato in goose fat is a healthy option, no matter how tasty it is.

The alarming factor in adjusting to French eating is learning to cope with the sheer number of courses that are served at each meal. Normally I only eat one course, especially at a restaurant, because I know that I won't be able to get through the quantity of food on offer. Here over days and weeks and months I have insidiously become accustomed to a more leisurely pace of eating that stretches over several hours and routinely includes six or seven courses. Time plays a big part in this ritual. No longer the fast snack of Sao biscuits with a thin slice of tomato eaten at the kitchen sink, or the quick one-course meal washed down with a glass of wine before a concert or a movie. Here I have all day and all night to enjoy lunch or dinner, and it's an easy habit to fall into. I guess my stomach simply stretches to accommodate the extra food.

There are hundreds of small restaurants around that specialise in traditional cuisine. Most of them are far from expensive—indeed the daily set menu is extremely reasonable considering that there are at least four or five courses, and that wine is generally included in the price. These restaurants are frequented during the week by truck drivers, road labourers and office workers who, in true French tradition, anticipate a large hot meal in the middle of the day. Many businesses and local councils issue their workers lunch vouchers so they can get their meal at a considerable discount, and this forms part of their pay package. At the weekends the customers are slightly different. Saturday lunch is popular with shoppers returning home from the markets at various small towns and villages. Sunday is the day for families to go out for a slap-up meal, and the menu varies accordingly. Instead of the set weekly menu, there are usually a few choices of main course and dessert at the weekend.

Our closest favourite restaurant is the only thriving business in Pomarède, and Jock is nervous about me broadcasting too many details of its existence, lest the good word spreads and it becomes too popular. His greatest fear is turning up for lunch and being told there are no tables left. Known as Madame Murat's, it is little more than a simple cottage by the side of the road that has been open for more than forty years, first run by Madame Murat's mother, currently by Jeanne Murat with the help of her daughter Sylvie, who will no doubt take over in ten years or so when Madame Murat runs out of steam. Madame Jeanne Murat is a short stout woman in a blue floral apron who produces vast quantities of excellent food at reasonable prices for her appreciative customers six days a week. The restaurant closes on Monday—the quietest day in rural France—but for the rest of the week it's packed every lunchtime. There are always a couple of pigs out the back waiting to be turned into roast pork, pâté and sausage, and everything on the menu is made in the small but well laid-out kitchen—all the soup stocks and pastries and sauces. During the busy summer months the kitchen throbs with heat and activity as groaning dishes are carried to the tables and extra bottles of wine are endlessly produced.

Carole, a bright, lively Englishwoman also works in the restaurant and, like most English-speaking locals, she is also a great mate of Jock. With her cockney husband Bob, Carole is an escapee from dreary 1980s London, who has adapted brilliantly to living and working in France. Bob and Carole's story is one of survival against the odds. They managed to buy a farmhouse within their limited budget but within weeks of settling in Bob fell head first over the handlebars of his bicycle, badly fracturing his skull. He nearly died and was in a critical condition for many months, leaving Carole and their two small sons with little savings and no prospect of an income. Although she spoke very little French, Carole managed to get a job in the kitchen of Madame Murat's and now, eight years later, she is an indispensable part of a team that keeps both the regular working population and holidaymakers supplied with mountains of terrific food. And now her French is fantastic. At the weekends she works with Bob on the continuing task of restoring their beautiful old farmhouse. Like all renovations it seems endless, and one that consumes every spare centime of their hard-won earnings.

At Madame Murat's, the traditional meal begins with a steaming bowl of potage or soup. A large soup tureen is brought to the table so that patrons can help themselves, and it's implicit that if the bowl runs dry there's always more. There is seldom a request, however, because people know what's coming next. In summer the soups are light, based on chicken stock with just a few fine vermicelli noodles and some tomato to flavour. In winter they are thicker, containing a range of hearty ingredients like turnips, broad beans, pumpkin, sorrel and sausage. At the village meals and fêtes, this soup may be a garlicky white broth with rough slices of bread thrown in at the last moment, and often containing a few eggs, the whites whisked and added separately from the yolks. It's not rich but very satisfying, and in truth, if combined with perhaps a second course of cheese, it would be more than enough for the average lunch or dinner appetite. At Madame Murat's the soup is even more satisfying. But it's only just the beginning.

The entrée, often called the charcuterie course, can take many forms. Slices of dark pink ham served with a cube of unsalted butter and melon or dill pickle; rough terrine or pâté of foie gras; omelette with mushrooms; warm salad of duck gizzards; chunks of various sausages combined with mounds of grated carrot and other salad vegetables; ravioli with foie gras; goat cheese pie; or potato and ham pancakes. At this point you really should get up from the table and leave, quite satisfied. But you don't because the main course is looming.

Chicken or duck, veal or beef, lamb or rabbit, wild boar or pork. You name it and Madame Murat's has developed a mouth-watering way of cooking it. The plat, or main course, is generally a meat dish with potato, or occasionally couscous or pasta, and maybe one lone vegetable dish. The concept of a dinner plate piled with a range of vegetables accompanying the main recipe is absolutely un-French. I have even seen diners at Madame Murat's serve themselves the vegetable—in this case a juicy tomato stuffed with pork and herbs—onto the side plate, eating the meat and potatoes first, then eating the tomato separately. It's as if the three dishes could not possibly be combined on one plate. Sauces are always rich and tasty, and bread is used throughout the meal to soak up all the juices and gravies, and to help shovel the food onto the fork which in turn is shovelled into your mouth. It's a good idea to undo the top buttons of your pants at this stage.

To cleanse the palate a salad is usually produced after the plat. It can be quite plain—just green leaves and dressing—or enriched with crisp leaves of endive or whitlof or various grated vegetables. Pause for breath because the cheese is about to arrive, with more crispy bread, par naturellment.

What can I say about French cheese? It's difficult not to eat a lot of it. I keep thinking that if I skip the cheese course I might stop putting on weight, but sometimes it's impossible to let the platter pass by. Madame Murat's, like most restaurants, arranges a variety of soft and hard cheeses on a bed of vine leaves, and the aroma when it is placed on the table is irresistible. But I find even the mass-produced supermarket cheeses mind-blowingly good. The cheese wagons at the open markets can be a bit daunting—literally sixty or seventy varieties to choose from— but if you can learn and identify just a handful of good varieties you will be happy for life. I wonder if I perhaps skip the other courses and the wine and just eat the cheese I will be okay. But without red wine the cheese is nothing, so what the hell.

By the time dessert arrives I have generally stopped caring, and listen intently to the choices. Crème brûlée with its creamy custard and crust of toffee is hard to pass up, as are the various ice-creams and sorbets. Rich pastry tarts are always divine, with the fruit varying according to the season—plums in spring and in late summer, apple. Clafoutis is another regional speciality, basically fruit covered with a rich cake-like matter that is then baked in the oven. There is also a pastry pie called pastis which I try not to miss.

My regular restaurant and café lunches are generally instigated by my small group of single male friends which includes Claude, a retired English photographer with an interesting, if chequered, background. Claude is Polish by birth and Italian by descent, but educated in England where he worked for forty years as a fashion photographer before coming to live full time in the Lot. Claude has one of the best houses I've seen in these parts—a renovated millhouse over a stream with a fantastic converted barn which he lets out as a holiday rental in the summer, plus a sumptuous adjoining house for himself. His garden is also to die for—it's been designed by Margaret Barwick and is planted and maintained by Philippe and Jan. It includes a formal garden and a croquet lawn; wild areas planted with colourful deciduous trees; a natural pond and a swimming pool; an orchard and a near-perfect small potager adjoining a glasshouse.

Claude also has a small flock of wild ducks that have settled permanently in the mill stream that flows along the side and then underneath his house. He feeds them daily with grain and carefully chopped cubes of bread, to the point where they have become dependent on his generosity. When he travels, Claude needs a duck-sitter—a task which I cheerfully volunteer to perform for ten days while he is holidaying in northern England. Living in his spacious house after months of being in my tiny room with a loo is luxury indeed, and I revel at suddenly having a dishwasher, a washing machine and a television that gets more than fifty international channels. Claude also has a terrific stereo so I can play loud classical music and opera as I sip wine and gaze at the sun setting over his dappled woodland, or watch the antics of the ducks through the floor-to-ceiling picture windows.

All the luxuries that I take for granted at home somehow seem more appealing after several months without them. Yet, living without them hasn't been at all difficult, in fact I have thoroughly enjoyed paring my life back to a few simple basics. Now, while I'm finding a house filled with modern conveniences enjoyable, I realise it's by no means essential for survival. And in many ways Claude's house seems alien to me, being so large and luxurious with six bedrooms, five spacious bathrooms and numerous living and dining areas. Claude lives here on his own for most of the year, rattling around from room to room, and I can't help but recall how our family of seven, including my mother and four children, survived quite cheerfully with one bathroom and one toilet for more than twenty years. Quite primitive by comparison.

The day before Claude returns from his holiday I am awoken at 4.30 in the morning by loud banging and crashing at the front door, followed by repeated ringing of the electronic bell. It is raining heavily. Through the glass doors I see a group of agitated men dressed in heavy black wet-weather gear, totally drenched and looking rather pathetic. I quickly realise that it's the Pompiers as they shout through the door that they need to use the telephone to get assistance to the scene of a nasty car accident a little further down the road. They have a mobile phone, but this stretch of road is somehow out of the network's range and they have been unable to get a connection. They enter, dripping across Claude's beautifully polished floors, and once the lights go on they take in the splendour of the house, especially the gorgeously decorated kitchen. There are many 'Oohs' and 'Aahs' and 'Très jolie cuisine, Madame' as they admire their surroundings while one of them makes the life-saving phone call. As quickly as they arrived, they troop soggily out into the rainy dark of early morning, and after I snuggle back into my bed, I wonder if I dreamt what just occurred. When I see the wreck of the car at the local garage later that day, I realise that I didn't.

When Claude returns we grab Jock and go to Madame Murat's, of course, for a reunion lunch. I laugh at how easily I am persuaded to join the boys in this huge midday feast, but ratio-nalise my weakness by saying that I am only trying to live the life of a local. After all, eating wonderful food is one of the main reasons why people from all over the world visit France, and it seems crazy to resist while I am here. Those who have been around for a while and those who now live here full time say that eventually you get over the novelty of such large meals and settle back into a more normal eating pattern so that balance is restored. I certainly like to think I would.

21

ALL THROUGH MY LIFE MY body size and shape has fluctuated according to what I am doing at the time. When flat out and stressed I trim down; when relaxed, pregnant or on holiday and feeling cruisy, I plump up. This time I have plumped up big time. Seven or eight kilos in a couple of months, and people are starting to comment.

My more polite friends say, 'You've changed quite a lot since you arrived.' The more direct, like Margaret, say, 'Just look at your thighs and hips.'

I haven't got a full-length mirror in Villefranche which is just as well, but I can notice the extra chin I am now carrying. And when I look downwards I can see a sizeable belly. A middle-age spread. A French roll. The dramatic change of lifestyle—no work, not a lot of gardening and wicked five-course meals—is the obvious cause and I am faced with some grim alternatives. Diets are a waste of time. It's either get into an exercise regimen or just cut back on the eating and drinking. I opt for the exercise.

To my mind walking is the least painful way of exercising, but it can be boring if you walk the same way day after day. Here, of course, there is so much of interest to see that walking will be a pleasure and I plot several routes out of the village that will give me an hour of pounding the roadside every day. The weather is still blazing hot, so early morning is the best idea. I have some good walking sandals and shorts, even though I have to expose those flabby bits around my knees. Like most bastide towns, Villefranche is set on a hillside so I can walk down towards the market gardens, where the local women are harvesting vegetables before the sun rises high in the sky. They wave as I stride past, looking a little curiously at my determined gait. I am walking on small back roads which are paved but narrow, and if a car or white van comes by, I must step into the roadside ditch. Not really a problem.

The last part of the walk, up the steep hill into the lower side of the village, brings me out in a healthy sweat so I arrive home bright red in the face and ready for a meagre shower in my tiny cupboard. I also do some stretching exercises, some full knee bends and sit-ups. It all helps a little, and although I don't actually drop any kilos, I seem to reach a plateau.

I begin to wonder if losing weight at this stage of my holiday is really so important anyway. Is it just that I am feeling uncomfortable in my clothes, or is there a deeper reason for my feeling anxious about this sudden change of shape? I have always had rather an ambivalent attitude towards my body. In truth I have never regarded it as my best asset. During early adolescence I was teased by my father about my emerging shape, being the classic Irish female with a flat chest, broad hips and generous backside. I was terribly jealous of my slim-hipped, large-breasted girlfriends, especially at the beach where they looked so gorgeous in their skimpy bikinis. Not only did I not have the prerequisite bosom and boyish hips, but my pale skin simply burned, blistered and freckled, creating an overall effect that was a long way from the sixties surfie beachgirl image I so desperately desired. Those friends who had mousy brown hair simply bleached it blonde to complete the scenario, while I was stuck with a tight frizz of bright red curls. It was all too humiliating.

Having a poor body image helped me to remain a virgin for much longer than my contemporaries. Not only did boys not compete to conquer me, I was reluctant for any of them to actually see me naked, so in one way being 'unattractive' in my own eyes did have some long-term benefits. While my girlfriends were busy sneaking out their bedroom windows at night for illicit trysts in the backseats of cars with spotty members of the local football team, I was not even vaguely aware that such activities were a possibility. I didn't have my first period until I was sixteen, so I remained quite naive and childlike long after other girls around my age were embarking on their sixth or seventh serious sexual affair. When I finally did become sexually active, not long before my eighteenth birthday, I still felt very uncomfortable about my flat chest and lumpy hips. I had a series of unsatisfactory relationships which I am sure were the result of my insecurity about my body. I was not particularly sporty, but I loved swimming and sailing and was always active, getting enough exercise at the weekends to remain reasonably fit and trim. My shape was pure genetics, not the result of too little exercise or too much fatty food. I just had to live with it.

I became more relaxed and accepting of my body shape in my early twenties, but the first time I ever really thought I looked beautiful when unclothed was when I was about six months pregnant with Miriam. I caught a glimpse of myself in the full-length mirror on my way to the shower, and saw my curved hips and belly in quite a different light. It took my breath away. I actually had breasts for the first time, and pale pink nipples that were full and ripe. David also adored my new pregnant shape, and constantly stroked my rounded tummy and full bottom and told me I was gorgeous. I believed him, and this probably helps explain why I took to pregnancy and mother-hood with such great enthusiasm. At last my body was doing what it was shaped for. Not parading for the lustful eyes of surfies at the beach but carrying a child. The fact that my body then performed brilliantly during the birth, doing all that was expected without complication, also lifted my self-esteem and confirmed my belief that my body was finally serving me well.

In my late twenties and thirties, when I became seriously involved in gardening, my body became strong and flexible in a way that again was very satisfying. Years of lifting toddlers onto my hips, chopping wood for the fires, lugging great bags of manure to the garden beds, digging and barrowing and working in all weathers gave my body a power and strength. In spite of my fairness, my arms and legs became quite tanned and tough, although I now protected my freckled face with lots of creams and broad-brimmed hats. The breasts I had developed during my various pregnancies and when feeding my babies didn't disappear or turn into pancakes, instead they remained quite firm and perky.

My mother had always been and always remained very thin. I suspect it was her terrible smoking habit that caused her appetite to dwindle more and more as she grew older. As a young woman in photographs she always seemed unnaturally thin to me, with dark circles under her eyes. And the few grainy snapshots of her when we were little, especially those taken after baby Jane died, show a woman who looks as though she has just been released from a concentration camp. For me, my mother's thinness was a legacy of her ill-health and the hardship of her life, and so I never aspired to be like that. I was happy in mid life to have my own shape, but to be fit and well-muscled at the same time.

In France, without my normal busy physical schedule, the weight that I gain so rapidly is more flab than muscle. I don't like the appearance of the extra chin in the mirror, and I hate the belly that I can't suck in, no matter how hard I try. I just don't feel comfortable in my own skin, which is why I am trying so valiantly to shed at least a couple of kilos here and there. I am gradually accepting that while I lead this carefree lifestyle I am bound to be well-padded. It's such a small price to pay for so much fun. Then through careful observation I realise that French women simply don't eat the same quantities that I have been so happily devouring. They do participate in every course, but always have a modest serving of each. Not several large ladles of soup and second helpings of pommes frites. So I gradually modify my eating habits and discover that I am more than full at the end of every meal. Not groaning with overload as I get up from the table, as I have done before.

I am certainly thankful that in our family eating food has always been a pleasurable activity, and not one tinged with guilt or anxiety about weight gain. Several young contemporaries of my daughter have had serious problems with eating disorders and I wonder if their own mothers' attitudes to food and eating have had a negative effect. Miriam and I both love our food and derive a lot of pleasure from planning and cooking meals for the family. She too has weight that fluctuates, but seems to have a healthy attitude towards her shape.

For the entire time I stay in Villefranche I keep up my daily walking regimen. It not only helps clear my head of cobwebs caused by too much of the high life, it introduces me to the tremendous range of local flora that crowds the roadsides. The small things you see when walking simply can't be appreciated from a car, especially if you are the driver. As I walk from the centre of the village the views on all sides are a delight. Fields crammed with maize and old farmhouse buildings in various stages of decay. There is always a strong fragrance and looking downwards I see my feet are crushing plants along the roadside. There are wild mints, including corn mint and pennyroyal, which release abundant aromas when I crush them between my fingers or walk on them. There are also several dainty purple-blue salvias, including *Salvia pratensis* or meadow clary, which produces tall slender flowerheads that pop up through other wild weeds. Wild yarrow is growing everywhere, with its dainty, small white flowerheads and ferny foliage that forms a richly fragrant mat at ground level. Other perfumed delights I stumble across on my walks include wild basil which has bright pink blooms and foliage with an intense aroma; various wild thymes including the common *Thymus praecox*; clumps of sweet-smelling marjoram; and sprays of callamint with mauve flowers and aromatic foliage. As I walk I train my eye to pick out plants that at home would be part of a perennial border or formal herb garden; it's often hard to distinguish them growing in the wild because they are much smaller and often jostle for space between grasses and other wild plants. Blackberry, such a noxious weed at home, is in its element here and grows down every country laneway, offering rich sweet fruits to be gathered in summertime. It's a nuisance here too, of course, because it catches and tears your clothes as you walk by and can easily invade the precious fields and meadows if not kept in check. But I must keep in mind that here they are not an introduced menace, instead a natural plant that just needs to be kept under control. Common buddleia is also omnipresent, having found its way here from China some centuries ago; it springs up against every wall and in every crevice, and has a charming habit of attracting butterflies by the hundred when in full bloom.

Over several months of walking I identify dozens of wild plants in flower, and my gardening friend, Pam, lends me several excellent English-language reference books to help me confirm my guesses at the species. I gather large bunches of those in flower and those with distinctive perfumes, and take them back to my small room where they fill the warm night air with a rich mix of aromas. There are various evening primroses (*Oenothera* sp.) with tall stems and blowsy yellow flowers, which I am surprised to learn are all of American origin, having arrived some hundred or more years ago and followed their habit of spreading like wildfire across the countryside. There are mallows (*Malvea* and *Lavatera*) everywhere, in gardens as well as along the country lanes, and they are a charming addition to the natural landscape with their profuse pink, white or mauve flowers. I also identify several species of *Silene*, commonly known as campion or catchfly, and am fascinated to read that there are eighteen species, quite a few native to this region. I love their inflated calyxes, which in some instances dominate the petals to become the main feature of the plant. As the season progresses the plants in flower change, and in later summer I will find wild sweet peas, the showy white angelica, and banks of purple heather; these I try to identify in the more comprehensive guides without success, but eventually I track them down in a local French wildflower guide as *Erica carnea*, or Bruyère des Neiges, which translates as heather of snow, because it originates in the Alpes Maritimes. It's a truly beautiful small plant which has naturalised down grassy roadside banks, generally in half shade.

When I finally move from Villefranche it's to be near the woods, and I anticipate many more walks and botanical discoveries. But my walking days are seriously curtailed. It's not through laziness, but because of the start of the hunting season which makes casual country walking, especially in the woods, a hazardous experience. I am still able to take sunny walks around the fields that lie on the south side of the house, but any sauntering into the woods or even along the side of the road is risky; the hunters are constantly stalking prey, and all too often mistake innocent walkers for a wild boar or deer. My nervousness about the anarchistic way in which the hunts are conducted drives me back inside as the weather cools, except for Wednesdays when the hunt is forbidden. This is the one weekday when children are home from school, and previous mishaps have demonstrated that children and hunters on the loose at the same time are not a good combination.

22

ONCE JULY AND AUGUST ARE over and most of the summer holidaymakers have gone back home to England or Holland or Paris, my chances of renting something slightly larger at a reasonable rate suddenly improve. There's talk among our friends about the opportunities to do some housesitting in the autumn and winter because so many part-time residents leave their country abodes deserted for six months at a stretch, and are more than happy for someone to keep an eye on things as long as they contribute towards the running costs and maintain the garden. But the one strong possibility on that score falls through at the last moment when the owners hint that they'd also like quite a substantial rental—something I can't really justify given my limited budget. Realistically I don't need a four-bedroom house, especially if it is going to cost a fortune.

My friend Carole from Madame Murat's comes to the rescue. She and Bob have friends at Pomarède—Olav and Hannah from Denmark—who have inherited a small stone cottage in the woods from Olav's father. They can only visit the property four or five weeks a year, four in the summer and one in autumn. During the last autumn while the house was lying empty, their gardening tools were stolen from the barn, so they are delighted at the prospect of somebody minding it for three months. The rental is still within my budget—2,000 ff ($500) a month plus electricity, although I will need to get firewood for the open fires, for it's certain to start getting rather cold in October.

Pomarède is on the way to the shopping township of Prayssac, and it's a route I travel often, whizzing past Madame Murat's popular restaurant. Lucienne also lives in the village, which is little more than a collection of old stone houses, a church and a mairie (town hall) which is in the process of having an halle de fête (festival hall) added for the regular summer parties and celebrations. No matter how small, all the villages seem to want their own hall as a sort of status symbol—some of them are quite grand and would have been costly—even if they are only used half a dozen times a year. The new hall in Pomarède looks as though it will tower over all the other buildings, and it's a cause of some controversy within the village. My little house in the woods is only a couple of minutes from the village as the crow flies, but feels much further away because it is reached through such a series of winding back roads that it takes a few visits to memorise. Once you leave the main road and start weaving through these tiny country lanes you get a sense of being in 'deep' France.

Carole drives me through these winding country lanes to find the little cottage which is completely hidden from the road by dense chestnut woods. There is a cleared field out in front, but on three sides it is overwhelmed by tall trees that cast long dark shadows in the autumn light. The house is a typical small farming or woodcutter's cottage: one main room with a vast open fireplace where once all the cooking would have been done and a stone sink for washing up, and one smaller room plus a loft where the tobacco crops once grown so widely in the area would have been dried. To one side is an annexe with two very small rooms that would have been the original pigsties. This area has been enclosed with a log cabin style extension, and the pigsties have been converted into a kitchen and a bathroom. So I've gone up-market. From a kitchen tucked under the stairs and a loo inside a wardrobe to a couple of rustic renovated pigsties. Even though this little house is isolated and could become gloomy during the colder months, the fact that it has a garden and a place to sit out and enjoy what remains of the balmy weather is enough to convince me it will be just perfect for my needs. Having lived in a township and then in the countryside I will have experienced the best of both worlds: village life with bars and restaurants and stray cats, and country life with open fires and wild woods on all sides.

However, before packing up and leaving my small room in Villefranche-du-Périgord I decide to throw a party to thank all my new friends for their unstinting hospitality. It can be quite embarrassing being asked out for dinner repeatedly, and not being in much of a position to return the favour. With a kitchen so small and inadequate, a tiny table, and a toilet inside a cupboard, it's hardly a suitable venue for elaborate dinner parties. But a farewell cocktail party with nibbles and wine should be well within my scope, so I pick a day and start making up a guest list. To my surprise I realise there are more than thirty-five people I would like to invite, and I wonder how on earth I am going to squeeze them into such a small space—with only three chairs and a bed for sitting down. Someone also warns me that some of the people on my list don't necessarily mix socially, that there are various groups within the group and that I had best not have them all together. I decide to totally ignore this bit of advice, because I don't intend throwing two parties just to satisfy some quirky social hierachy. They will all have to cope, and so will I.

My guest list includes an eclectic bunch of new friends ranging in age from three to eighty-six. The three-year-old is the grand-daughter of Jock's part-time neighbours, Andy and Sue Greif who are also friends of the Barwicks and who have been drawn to the region after making several visits on holiday. In their former lives Andy was a colonial police officer posted to Tonga, Kenya and the Caymans, and after retirement they tried hard to settle down in the UK but found the weather quite impossible after decades of tropical living. They now divide their time between France and Spain—winters in the sparkling heat of Alacante, and summers in the Lot at the time of year when Spain becomes impossibly hot and overcrowded with tourists. They are a good-looking couple who love having people in for drinks, an impromptu game of boules or a meal in the garden. Sue is an accomplished artist and also an animal lover—she has adopted two gorgeous village cats in Spain and brought them to St Caprais for the summer. Their daughter is visiting from England along with her two small children, and will still be here for my party.

The eighty-six-year-old is Godfrey, a fellow resident of Ville-franche, also English and also retired. His wife Joyce, affec-tionately known around the traps as 'Joyce the Voice', is one of those people who cannot abide a nanosecond pause in the conversation, and who has taken it upon herself to make sure that a social gaffe such as a pause for breath never occurs. Her jaw is like lightning, zapping up and down and filling the air with all sorts of information that is of no interest to those unfortunate enough to be the target of her tongue. Her favourite subjects are her family and her friends, very few of whom anyone has ever actually met, mostly only known by name, but Joyce does not let this stop her. Her penchant for detail means you must also be told about the offspring of her family and friends, and in intimate detail. Especially their academic achievements and personal triumphs. It's exhausting.

I first encounter Joyce at a drinks party. No more than five feet one inch, she is grasping her wine and nailing her victim with nonstop details of her grandson's latest examination results. She then talks to me for twenty minutes about her sister's husband's niece's brilliant career and after it I am left wondering who the hell she is talking about. At the communal lunches and dinners people fight openly about who has to sit next to Joyce, and it is generally organised so that unsuspecting newcomers take the honours.

Godfrey, on the other hand, maintains an air of quiet irritation combined with a certain resignation. After a few glasses of wine, however, he starts taking swipes about her verbal dexterity, and if she's in earshot, things can get lively indeed.

'My two worst problems in life are being eighty-six and being married to Joyce,' he once whispers in my ear, but not very effectively because he's deaf and tends to shout.

'What was that you said, Godfrey?' says Joyce, having heard every syllable. 'Very funny, I must say. I hope YOU find him amusing, my dear.'

Even though Joyce can be exasperating, as a couple they can be good value and I really want to invite them along to my party, so I call in at their house unannounced late one afternoon. What I intend as a quick visit is *so* exasperating, I almost wish I hadn't come.

'It's on Wednesday the tenth. Six pm. Bring your own glass.'

Quite simple I would have thought. But first a cup of tea then Joyce consults her diary. An opportunity to expound on the intricacies of her life. She begins two weeks ahead of my proposed party and tells me about the visitors she is expecting on the twenty-fourth.

'Godfrey's nieces are coming for four days, or is it five? Is it five, Godfrey? I can't quite read what I've put down here. They're coming from Canada, of course, because their parents went there in 1940. She was a brilliant girl, of course, and could have done a lot better if things had been different, and he was a scientist of some note. They lived there for twenty-three years before moving to the Middle East where the children went to school. Well only the youngest, Brian, the others were at college and later they went on to a special university, of course, because they could speak three languages, and her sister also had three children and the last one was a girl. She said later that if she had known it would be a girl she wouldn't have bothered because the boys were both so good, you know. And the girl was hard work. Although I think one of them had motor problems. Motor problems, wasn't it, Godfrey? Anyway they are coming from Geneva and it will take about nine hours, it's a long day, and my problem is how to get all the beds changed because they will overlap with Jeremy. And he never says how long he's staying and I have to organise the beds because then there's Leo and his friend Joe who are staying in an old house in Brieve with eighteen friends. They've just finished their Bach exams and Leo did very well, which was hard for him because he took French and after all those years at the other college he found things very hard indeed.'

Eventually, after fifteen minutes or more of this, Joyce rolls back the diary to the week in question, unfortunately not to the Wednesday, but to the Monday before.

'Now this is going to be interesting,' and she launches off again. Who will be staying with them over the preceding weekend. The relatives of those staying. The achievements of their children, and, I think, their nieces and nephews. I'm not too sure because I have stopped listening about twenty minutes ago.

Eventually I summon some courage. 'But what about the Wednesday? Can you come?' I ask lamely.

'That should be absolutely fine,' says Joyce, and scrawls it in her diary.

The date finalised and the friends formally invited, I plan a simple menu. I will slice up baguettes and top them with mounds of egg mayonnaise, caviar and smoked salmon. I will track down some excellent pâté and cheese and also layer this onto crusty bread. It's far easier for people to cope with finger food if it isn't large and messy, but can be put in the mouth in a single bite. The cats look very interested in all this food preparation, especially the enticing smell of the salmon, so I need to close the windows and doors until just before the party starts as there is nowhere to hide food platters from their greedy clutches. The day I have chosen turns out to be the hottest day in August, more than 40 degrees, with the afternoon sun belting directly onto my shutters. I clear the furniture back against the wall as much as possible, chill the wine and beer and make a big bowl of Australian-style punch with pineapple juice, rum and chopped-up fruit.

Everyone seems to arrive at once and as most people know each other, introductions are not required. Before long I have twenty-nine hot and sweaty visitors crammed into my tiny room, although they soon spill out into the corridor and onto the street. My landlord looks a bit alarmed and kindly offers to bring over some extra chairs—he even generously suggests we all move across the road into his walled garden. I don't imagine he ever anticipated this tiny room being a major party venue. However everyone is having fun and even the cats have joined in, skulking around in corners looking for odd scraps of food. Luckily there is a public toilet just a few doors away, so nobody is required to brave my prefab thunderbox. By the time it gets dark the hangers-on decide they are still hungry, so we all wander through the back streets to a restaurant that specialises in thin, crispy pizzas. Next morning my room looks somewhat shattered but the memories of the party are sweet so I don't resent mopping up the aftermath. That same day I start packing for the move from Villefranche to Pomarède.

23

 THE DAY I MOVE HOUSE IT'S A stifling 40 degrees, and very humid. I am really keen to get settled in quickly because I have discovered that there was once a phone line to the cottage and Lucienne has helped me organise with France Telecom to have it reconnected. I will move in the morning and the phone will be linked up between 3 and 5 pm. I am anxious to have a phone because Lorna's baby still hasn't arrived, it's now more than a week overdue. When I moved from Jock's place to Villefranche my possessions easily fitted into the boot of the car, with a few clothes on hangers in the back seat. I can't work out why this move is going to take at least two full car loads. But there are the contents of the fridge and pantry shelf, including half a dozen or so bottles of wine, tinned food and bottles of spirits left over from the party. There's the bedding from Margaret and Jock, the electric wok, a borrowed sewing machine, plus some extra bits and pieces I have bought since I first moved in. It's a sad fact of life that no matter where you live you manage to accumulate all sorts of stuff. I even a have small basket of odd bits and pieces like stickytape, batteries, toothpicks and birthday candles—just like I have at home. How did it happen?

After I settle I find the main problem with the house in the woods is that it's dark—very dark indeed. The attic room, which has been converted into the only real bedroom, has no window at all, just stone walls and a wood-lined pitched roof with heavy timber beams. Although appealing in a rustic way, walls of natural stone and timber ceilings with heavy beams simply absorb the light. Even when several lamps are glowing it still feels dark and gloomy. In many of the renovated houses around here the owners have wisely painted the timber between the beams pure white with uplights to brighten the interior. However in my little cottage in the woods it's all very natural and old-fashioned, and extremely dim. I cannot read a book even in the middle of the day. Most old stone cottages also lack windows and doors, which would let out too much heat in winter. The Petersens have put candles everywhere, hanging chandeliers of them in the dining area, and placing huge candle stands on either side of the open fireplace in the living room. It's certainly a romantic effect for the evenings but I know that I will need light, for reading and sewing, and also for my mood. Rooms that are dark during the day are depressing, especially when the weather is cold and the sky is overcast. I hate overhead lighting which is often oppressive, preferring lamps scattered through the rooms and realise I may have to buy a few more. I know that the fire will add greatly to my good humour and that I will probably start lighting it in the evenings long before it becomes really cold.

The gas bottle needs to be connected for the stove and hot

water, and this is done by a sunny-natured stocky chap called Florent. He has been employed by the Petersens as a sort of general factotum—he drops around to keep an eye on security when they are not here, mows the lawns and does any odd jobs that are required. He is to be my helper if I get into strife. I offer him a cold beer after he's hooked up the appliances, and he drinks it with great enthusiasm. When he leaves he kisses me goodbye and it's quite an experience. He is a good deal shorter than me but he clasps me firmly by the shoulders and drives his face against my cheek, kissing with a vigorous sucking action. Instead of the usual two light cheek pecks he gives me four hearty sucks, and this greeting and farewell is repeated every time he calls in. Which is often. I have to brace myself for the warmth of his embraces.

The little house suddenly starts to breathe with life when I open the shutters and clean the windows. I vacuum away the layers of dust and cobwebs and install the paraphernalia I now carry to 'set dress' my budget abodes. The tablecloth, the pretty bedcovers and the lamps all look well, but I definitely need some extra lamps to brighten up the place, especially a strong halogen for reading, writing and sewing. A bunch of flowers from Carole's on the kitchen table, a bottle of wine on the ice, and I am set. I love doing a bit of an interior makeover. It probably stems from the days of my messy childhood, when I frequently dashed around tidying up after the rest of the family. I have a dreadful tendency to sweep things off surfaces into drawers to get rid of unwanted clutter, which means that I often cannot find things when I need them. However I do have a strong sense of maintaining order in my life. For me a house must be clean, light and warm, preferably with the smell of something wonderful cooking on the stove. I love flowers from the garden and comfortable places to sit. This little stone house can fulfil most of those requirements. In fact, I can't wait for a cold day so that I can light the fire in the vast fireplace that dominates the main room.

There are many empty houses in this part of France, either closed up for months of the year because their owners are overseas, or simply left to rot by their proprietors for various reasons: sometimes an inheritance dispute with several members of one family unable to agree whether to occupy or sell; sometimes the families really don't need the money and would prefer the house to fall down rather than sell to an outsider. They figure that one day their grandchildren will inherit the property, but sadly, many of the younger generations—living in Toulouse, Paris or even further afield—have no real interest in occupying or restoring a house in such a remote place. In Frayssinet I notice that at least half the houses surrounding the main roads are permanently shuttered, with roof tiles showing signs of neglect and walls buckling. The village once had two bars and a whole row of busy shops along the main street. Now there is only the post office, one bar, and three food shops. Better than many villages, but at any stage one of these could close through lack of business, because so many of the homes are empty.

It was hard saying goodbye to Villefranche and my cats, especially Pierre, but it is sheer delight to be here in the countryside. Having some extra space to move around in gives me a sense of liberation, while having a garden where I can 'sit out' is a real luxury. The garden is little more than a rough-mown lawn and shrubs bordered by woods, with two large fields that were once used for grazing and crops. The owners have planted some shrubs at random in the fields, but they are struggling through lack of water. I yearn to dig them up and bring them all together in a single bed where they can be tended more easily; apart from anything else, they look totally out of place plonked in the middle of a field, and mowing around them must be a nightmare for Florent. However it is not my garden to interfere with, and I simply drag hoses to the unhappy plants and give them a long soaking whenever the weather gets really hot. The view of the fields is somewhat impeded by some badly located conifers that tend to close the house in and add to the darkness inside. Oh for a chainsaw . . .

Florent finds a table, umbrella and chairs for me, which I position on the lawn outside the kitchen window. I can now sit out for hours, even bringing my computer out onto the table. I ask various friends to pop around for a drink, and enjoy having some space for entertaining. People are much more likely to 'drop in' than when I was living in my tiny room. I expect it was like calling on someone in their bedroom rather than in a house with a proper front door.

Now that I have enough space to invite a few people around, I start organising some dinners. There are just so many wonderful ingredients to experiment with, and I have missed the ritual pleasure of cooking and serving meals for people, something I do almost every day at home. I try out the new stove, first cooking a lunch for Lucienne and Margaret and David Barwick who are about to spend six weeks away visiting their daughter in America and their son and grandchildren in the Cayman Islands. I then invite five men for dinner: Jock, Claude, Anthony, Roger and Danny. I spend the whole day shopping and cooking, casseroling rabbit and bacon in red wine and making my favourite Spanish entrée of chorizo sausage and poached eggs. It's a meaty, blokey meal and they all wolf it down. I thoroughly enjoy playing hostess to a bunch of unattached men.

The woods around the cottage are curious, with multi-trunked chestnuts lining the deep driveway into the property and continuing outwards, mingled with the occasional oak and pine. My first walk through the dappled woodland reveals the awful truth. These were once majestic stands of huge chestnuts that have been sheared through at ground level then simply allowed to reshoot from the base, producing up to ten spindly trunks. They still bear nuts but the entire character of the forest is changed. When I see the occasional old chestnut that has been left from the initial clearing, I can visualise how this area must have once looked. The French normally pride themselves on their forest management, but this looks like mismanagement to me. I would love to have seen new chestnut saplings planted after the clearing, to develop the same wonderful shape as the previous trees, but this would be a much slower and more costly option.

Mind you, there is virtually no original forest remaining anywhere in Europe, with the exception of some remote remnants at altitude. The woodlands around here are termed 'tertiary', which means they are at least three generations from the original cover, and probably bear little resemblance in terms of balance and diversity of species in comparison to what was once growing here. The clearing and destruction of these woodlands would have been well underway more than one thousand years ago, and over the centuries would have changed beyond recognition. In Australia we still have a small percentage of original bushland and forest, but Europe's mistake should teach us to clear no more, especially the old-growth forests that are a precious reminder of our botanical heritage.

One good thing is that the percentage of woodland here in southern France has greatly increased over the past one hundred years. Again, this is a symptom of the decline in population, with fewer farmers to work the land. And the phytophthora plague which devastated the vineyards in France on two separate occasions, has actually meant that land once cultivated has been allowed to regenerate as woods, which in turn has increased the bird and wildlife population.

But I am immediately in love with my woodland surroundings, even if they have been so badly bastardised. I listen and look for the birds and watch the changing scenery as the weather turns from summer into autumn.

I am still in my fairly laid back routine of sleeping late, doing a little writing in the morning, eating lunch, either in or out with friends, then falling into bed for an afternoon nap. Sleeping in the stone house is weird during the day because the bedroom, having no windows, is totally black. There's just a stairwell with a chink of light from a first-floor window. I awake from my afternoon sleeps feeling totally disorientated, wondering where I am and what time of day it is. I decide to try and change my lifestyle as winter approaches, for fear of turning into a bear and hibernating in the dark. I will forgo big lunches with wine, stay awake for all of the daylight hours, and go to bed early after enjoying a few hours by the open fire. More like the routine I have at home.

The house has a television and what appears to be a satellite dish against the back wall, weirdly pointing into a tree. But when I hook it all up, all I can get on the set are one or two local channels and even then the reception is very fuzzy. I decide that watching television may help improve my language skills, and I get into a routine of sitting with a notebook and jotting down new words, then looking up their meanings in my dictionary. Initially I just watch the news, but soon I am hooked on a couple of quiz shows and two very amusing reality programs. One is called 'Tous Egaux' and it features two very pretty studio hosts— one male, one female—who introduce a series of completely loony people who have two minutes to explain their particular and usually extremely odd passion—be it making unusual objets d'art out of recycled junk, playing the piano accordion while standing on their head, or belly dancing. The participants are totally earnest and they speak stacatto-fashion at the camera while performing. It is bizarre, but I find that after watching a few episodes, I can understand quite a bit of what they are saying. I assume it's because they are unsophisticated people whose use of language is fairly basic. Right up my alley.

The other is a more in-depth program called 'Striptease' which is a fly on the wall style of documentary on the lives of various people. Old drag queens, pigeon fanciers and other slightly eccentric members of the community. It's quite riveting and I always manage to get the general drift of what's happening. I later learn that this program has won several international television awards and I congratulate myself on my excellent taste.

On the whole, however, French television is fairly abysmal, as any French person will readily agree. I find it a comfort to have the television blaring from time to time, especially as background noise while I am cooking a meal. I have splashed out and bought a better quality radio that also plays tapes and CDs. I realise that I really missed hearing classical music while living in Villefranche—I grew up in a family where music was being played day and night. Silence, although soothing, can begin to grate after a few months.

At no time, either in Villefranche or in my little house in the woods, do I feel nervous about being alone, even in the dead of the night. Coming home late in the pitch black doesn't worry me in the slightest. I am not even vaguely concerned about locking up the house before I go to bed, although I always lock the doors before I go out—only because I have a brand new computer. I'm not a person with a vivid imagination when it comes to the possibility of danger from intruders—unlike my mother who spent her last few years incapable of being left alone at night. She wouldn't or couldn't sleep a wink if there wasn't another person in the house. I have been known to fall into bed leaving the front door not only unlocked, but actually open. I also reason that the crime rate in this part of the world is pretty low, and that I am therefore highly unlikely to become a victim. Having this relaxed attitude certainly gives me a great sense of freedom. If I were nervous, I suppose, I would never have chosen to live alone in a small stone house so isolated from its neighbours.

With the phone now connected I can ring home whenever I choose, and I do so more often than I really should. The line is amazing, I feel like I am just around the corner, ringing my darling daughter every couple of days as I would at home, calling David on location in Queensland, and checking in regularly to see how Aaron and Lorna are managing at home. I decide to sleep downstairs beside the telephone because Lorna's baby is now nearly two weeks overdue. I have a voicemail option on the phone which I use for storing messages, and check in every few hours in case I have missed the important call I am waiting for. I am feeling very strange about not being at home for the birth of this child, and am worried that when it finally happens I will be plunged into a depression. People are constantly asking me for any news of the birth, but the days drag on with nothing to report. Then late one night I come home from a dinner at Lucienne's to a frantic message from Miriam. Her voice is shaking with excitement and emotion.

'You have a granddaughter,' she sobs. 'Mum, Mum, it's a girl, it's a girl.'

I have a direct number for the hospital but I can't seem to get through immediately. After what seems like an eternity, but in reality is just a few minutes, I manage to track Miriam down in the delivery room. Lorna is exhausted, but the birth went brilliantly. No painkilling drugs, thanks to Miriam's ability to fend off the nursing staff, and one very lusty small girl who is to be called Ella Mary. I can hear her gurgling noises in the background, where Aaron is cuddling her while Lorna has a well earned rest.

After four boys it feels strange to think of myself as the grandmother of a girl. I am elated but also filled with a terrible hollow emptiness because I am so far away. I have always been actively involved in the arrival of my grandchildren, either assisting in the actual birth or doing all the practical things that are needed during the days and weeks after a baby is born. Now I am on the other side of the world and I can't participate in any practical or emotional way. I lie awake most of that first night, unable to sleep because of my excitement but also because I feel alienated. I don't feel the slightest twinge of guilt about not being there, but it is as though I have really missed out on something wonderful. I wonder how it will be greeting my granddaughter for the first time when she is three months old, instead of cradling her in my arms during those precious early days.

I am delighted for Aaron and Lorna that they have a daughter, and I hope that little Ella Mary will have as good a relationship with her mother as I had with mine, and as Miriam has with me. It makes me wish that Miriam also had a daughter, although she wouldn't swap her three bright-eyed boys for all the world. She isn't planning any more babies, so I guess this first little granddaughter will be it for quite some time. I'm looking forward to hunting down some georgous girlie baby clothes in the French shops and markets. Apart from that, there's nothing much I can do, except feel happy and excited. And more than a bit ashamed that I have been so busy partying that the cot quilt is still only half finished.

24

WHEN PLANNING THIS ESCAPE to France I imagined myself leaping around all over the countryside, visiting as many far-flung places as possible, probably crossing the borders into Spain and Italy, and making at least one trip to England to visit relatives in London. I studied maps and worked out how long it would take me to drive to these various locations, but never gave much thought to how I would fit so much gallivanting about into my schedule.

The weeks and months have passed quickly, all through the galloping summer festivities and into autumn. I realise that I have not ventured very far outside a fifty-kilometre radius of St Caprais, and that I have not seen very much of France at all, except for the southern tip of the Dordogne and the western tip of the Lot.

I can easily justify this lack of initiative by rationalising that instead of dashing hither and thither, I am living the life of a rural French woman. I am shopping and cooking and seeing friends and being part of the community, rather than being a tourist who flits from one place to another and only ever gets a superficial feeling for a country. Over years of travelling I know that staying put for a week or a month in one place results in a more memorable journey than a few days here and there, with a lot of packing of bags in between. But nevertheless I feel a need to leap outside my safety zone and do more exploring if I am to feel I have 'achieved' something during this six-month retreat.

Part of the problem is that sightseeing on your own is never really much fun, especially if the place you are visiting is exciting and you feel the desire to share some of that excitement with someone else. Around where I am living it's always easy to find someone to come along for a visit to more remote historic villages, or to touristy places like the underground river caves at Padirac or the ancient Christian pilgrimage cliff town of Roca-madour. But a trip further afield is more difficult to organise, which is why I haven't been doing more of them on my own.

I am told that there are 'sales' on in Toulouse and decide to visit. I will catch the train from Cahors which takes just over an hour, and stay overnight in a cheap hotel. I park my car at Cahors station to find the train is exactly on time, as they tend to be in France. The French so pride themselves on their transport timetables running to schedule that any passenger on a train more than thirty minutes overdue is entitled to a free ride of equal distance; it's a matter of honour. I arrive in Toulouse bright and early, and follow my guidebook to a tourist hotel in the middle of the shopping precinct. For less than 200 ff a night I have a very plain, windowless room with a hard bed and a huge bathroom. After months without a soaking bath I am momen-tarily excited until I realise the management has not provided a plug—obviously for such a low tariff they are not about to encourage guests to be lavish with the hot water.

Free of my overnight bag, I wander the back streets and numerous squares, but realise that few of the beautiful shops I have been told about actually open before 10.30 am. Time for a cup of tea and a quick read of an English newspaper before I start prowling the sales. The main problem I have is my new size and shape—I am reluctant to spend money on clothing that I cannot fit into and may never ever be able to fit into again. But I can't quite bring myself to buy clothes that are two or three sizes larger than my normal size.

However I love looking at the architecture of this wonderful city. Toulouse is commonly known as La Villa Rosa because of the pink coloured bricks that have been used for so many of the buildings. It's a university town, which gives it a youthful and vibrant atmosphere—quite the reverse of the low-key ambience where I have been living, where the average age is probably sixty-five. It is also a busy working city, not over-run with tourists and holidaymakers like Paris or Nice: it's easy to wander around without feeling like one of the hordes. I don't carry a camera and so I can even pretend that I'm a local.

Toulouse also has quite a large Vietnamese and Chinese population and I am easily able to track down a restaurant that serves Asian food, something I have been craving for weeks. Although I adore the food where I am living, I am accustomed to a more diverse diet, with at least one meal a week based on rice with stir-fried vegetables. Curiously, this restaurant has a set menu designed to appeal to the French custom of several small courses. Soup, and entrée, main course and dessert. No cheese, but otherwise an Asian-style Madame Murat's. However I opt for a bowl of combination soup with rice and a side dish, which is a little different to the way Asian food is prepared in Australia in that it seems a lot heavier, not as light and fragrant. But after a solid diet of duck and goose fat, it's heaven.

I have a short siesta after lunch, then hit the shops again with determination. I buy some sandals because at least my feet are the same size; a beautiful russet-coloured linen jacket that only feels a little tight across the shoulders; some scarves; and lots of glorious baby clothes in fine cotton fabrics. I also buy handmade animal puppets for the little boys, pack them carefully and post them back to Australia straightaway.

I opt for a light dinner then spend the evening sitting in a café in the Place Saint-George where crowds once used to gather for regular executions of religious martyrs. There is a pantaloon-wearing busker, naked to the waist, trying to earn some francs by breathing fire. He takes repeated swigs of kerosene from a bottle and lurches, spewing flames from table to table, terrifying patrons into handing over their coins to get rid of him. He is obviously extremely drunk. Some Americans at a nearby table are alarmed, but as one of my sons recently belonged to an amateur juggling and fire-breathing troupe, I am reasonably confident we are in no immediate danger, and soon the gendarmes appear and move him on. The Americans turn out to be a couple of rather refined art history experts on a university sabbatical, and fire-breathing drunks are not on their itinerary. I, however, am quite intrigued, as this busker is the first real drunk I have seen in France in more than five months.

Back in Pomarède I am still having trouble linking up to the Internet and I decide that I must upgrade my computer to a more modern piece of equipment. The French keyboard is set out quite differently to the English, which makes fast typing an impossibility. The only solution will be to go to England and buy one duty-free. My friend Anthony tells me he is planning to drive there the following week, and I ask if I can hitch a ride. I will gladly contribute towards the petrol and he says he'll be pleased of the company in the car—the trip from Pomarède to the ferry wharf at Caen is ten hours alone.

Anthony is a refugee from the financial bedlam of Hong Kong futures trading who found God and got divorced—I'm not sure in which order—and is gradually restoring a handsome stone house in Cassagne, near Pomarède, in an attempt to get his life back on a more even keel. Nothing like a major house renovation to bring a person back to earth with a thump. He has decided to undertake most of the work himself using a DIY handbook on house renovations and information gleaned from the Internet, and he seems to exist in a permanent maze of electrical cables, plumbing pipes and bags of cement. He has experienced some notable disasters—including a water pipe that burst in the middle of the night, drenching two floors of the semi-restored house—but finally seems to be getting into his stride with the assistance of one of Carole and Bob's strapping sons. Anthony's main hurdle is that he is too thoughtful for his own good. He analyses and agonises over every decision—the moral fabric of society, or whether or not to leave the fireplace intact or turn it into a storage cupboard. He's one of those people who are seekers of truth, who can't just take the world as it comes. Although my first impression of Anthony is one of quite an intense fellow, he turns out to be highly entertaining company when he can be inveigled into leaving his shambolic building site for a meal or a party.

Two days before we plan to leave for England he rings to

inform me about the sleeping arrangements on board the overnight ferry.

'We'll have to share a cabin,' he says a little sheepishly.

'What does that entail?' I am smiling to myself.

'There are two bunks, one on top of the other, and a shared bathroom.'

'Oh that's fine,' I quip. 'I've always preferred being on the bottom.'

Silence.

We plan to leave before midday and have a seafood dinner at the port before boarding the midnight ferry. The car journey to the coast is a long one, but not at all tedious. The countryside changes dramatically as we travel northwards, with the fields becoming much larger and flatter, without all the winding hedgerows and little villages of the south. The traffic becomes busier and scoots along much faster, even when we leave the motorway and start heading west towards the Normandy coast. Anthony and I seem to talk nonstop. He's a well-read man, with a broad general knowledge and a diverse range of interests that include history, music, philosophy and computers. Born in Africa, but raised and educated by his mother in England after his parents' separation, he has spent most of his adult working life in Hong Kong which is why he has never been able to settle back into the existence of an Englishman. The Lot suits him much better.

At Caen we leave the car in the queue and wander back from the wharf to find a pleasant seafood restaurant. We linger a while too long over a meal and dash back to our position as the cars and trucks are starting to board the ferry. Then we realise we have forgotten to do the essential paperwork at the check-in point, which means our car is now holding up the long queue behind it. It's all very embarrassing as the travellers in the queue behind have been waiting patiently inside their cars for their turn to board, while we have been sitting in a restaurant. On board at last, we head for the bar and a nightcap, where Anthony bumps into some friends. He decides to stay on in the bar for a while, and I head for bed, and am soon so soundly asleep that I don't hear him come back later. It's the first time I've shared a room with a man for many months, and I am not even really aware that he is there at all.

The bells ring at 5.30 am, allowing just enough time for a quick, greasy breakfast before driving the car off at Portsmouth. Anthony, who is looking slightly the worse for wear, drops me at Cambridge where I am to meet up with a rather zany but lovable woman called Bronte, whom I met when she was visiting the Barwicks in St Caprais. I warmed to her during her two-week stay, though I sensed she was a rather sad and lonely individual. When she heard I was coming to England she was very keen for me to visit. I am more than happy to spend a night in Cambridge because, apart from anything else, David's younger sister Gillian, who lives in London, is working flat out until the weekend and won't have a moment to spend with me before then.

Bronte also works, but she picks me up in the centre of town in the late afternoon and takes me back to her house. She has been living with the younger of her two adult sons and his girl-friend, but they are just in the process of moving to another city. It's all a bit chaotic but very warm and welcoming, and I quickly discover why Bronte is the only person I ever meet in France who doesn't drink one drop of alcohol: she is a bit of a dope fiend. Well, not exactly a fiend, but as I sit on her sofa hoping she may offer me a glass of something, instead she produces a fat joint. I'm rather over all that, so instead I suggest I take everyone out for a night at the local pub and a big English dinner. Bronte also doesn't seem to be keen on cooking, and the fridge looks rather bleak, so I figure it's my only chance of a drink and a feed.

Indeed we all have a splendid evening together, and are joined by her older son and his girlfriend. English pub culture and the food now served in pubs is rather pleasant, and a complete change from the southwest France cuisine and atmosphere. I thoroughly enjoy my fish and chips, and a couple of pints of good lager. Bronte is feeling low because, when her son moves the following day, she will be alone for the first time in more than twenty-five years. Her marriage failed many years back, but until quite recently she had a live-in lover who has since also departed. No wonder she is feeling sad. Living alone is all fine and dandy if you have a choice in the matter. This period of my life, in self-imposed exile, is causing me very little pain because I know that at the end of the six months I will be hopping on a plane and returning to the open arms of my large, warm family. For Bronte, who has a strained relationship with her mother, and two sons who are both now heading off in their own directions, the choices are much more limited. Being a woman of fifty without a partner is also problematic. The prospects of meeting someone congenial seems to narrow down with age, and working full-time to pay the bills means that life can become a grind of working and sleeping and little else.

In the morning I catch a train into London and am met at the station by David's sister Gillian and her daughter Annabel, who is just a few years older than Miriam. Gillian lived the life of a country housewife and mother in New Zealand for twenty-five years; then, after her marriage broke up, she launched into a career as a school matron and private nurse, making good use of her pre-marriage mothercraft nursing qualification. Several years back, in a dramatic contradiction of her conservative lifestyle, Gillian upped sticks and moved to London where she now works as a nanny and shares a flat the size of a postage stamp with a girlfriend called George, also from New Zealand. George has found work with a high-flying dot com company, and is also having a great time living and working in London. Annabel is visiting from New Zealand, working part time as a casual teacher at several alarmingly confronting comprehensive schools, and she is also camping in the tiny flat. She is sleeping on the sofa in the sitting room and I am to sleep on a futon bed at the other end of the room where our toes will virtually be touching during the night. Despite its ridiculous size, the flat costs them a fortune every week, hundreds of pounds for an area that is half the size of my garage at home. All three work long, gruelling hours, spending a second small fortune on train fares and food, but they still manage to save enough money get out of town regularly on long weekend holidays. Greece and France, Sweden and Scotland are just some of the places they have visited to escape the dreary weather and the expense of London.

We have a pub lunch and, while at the bar ordering beers, I suddenly catch a glimpse of the opening ceremony of the Sydney Olympics on the television monitor overhead. The games are one of the reasons I have chosen this particular six months to leave Australia behind, imagining that they will turn Sydney into a chaotic nightmare. However all the newspaper and television reports have been to the contrary, and now as I gaze up at the screen I feel a terrible wave of homesickness. When I see Cathy Freeman running with the Olympic torch towards the giant cauldron I am completely undone. How perfect that they—the much-ridiculed organisers—finally got it right, choosing this amazing young woman to complete the most important part of the ceremony. I stand sobbing in front of the screen while the others wait for me at our table.

'You all right, love?' the barman asks with some concern.

I am all right, but I suddenly feel that I am once again missing out on something very special at home.

Gillian and I only have three days together, and I have to buy my computer and also catch up with Miles and Anne, who are keen for me to stay a night and have dinner with some other friends who visited the Lot in July. And although I have been to England several times I have never done the tourist thing and seen the sights of London—Big Ben and the Houses of Parliament, Buckingham Palace. This is because David loathes the English class system with such a passion that he refuses to dignify the history of the city by visiting monuments that he considers are symbols of it. He has lived and worked in London on film projects several times over the years and felt he has been treated as a curious colonial, so this has greatly clouded his viewpoint. So Gillian, George and Annabel take me, via the tube, on a whirlwind tour of ten or more major tourist sites where I pose for a series of cheeky photographs, waving the Union Jack and grinning like Dame Edna Everage, to send to David back in Australia. I get plenty of funny looks from fellow tourists, especially when I hold a photograph of the Queen in front of my face while posing for my Buckingham Palace picture. I also indulge my love of kitsch by buying several Queen Mother plates and teapots to

take back to France. In the pastel blues and pinks of her fluffy
hats, they are truly hideous.

George drops me over to Miles and Anne's cosy terrace house
in Battersea for one night, and it's great to see them in their own
environment. Miles takes me to one of the clubs of which he has
been a long-time member, the Oxford and Cambridge Club, and
I am appalled to discover that women are still not permitted
to have a drink at the bar. I am only allowed to peek furtively
through the heavy oak portals to the overly grand male-only bar,
then we are forced to find a dreary backroom where men and
women can sit together. Given that more than half the students
of Oxford and Cambridge are female, I can't fathom how this
situation can still exist. Miles thinks it's mildly amusing, but Anne
and I agree that such sexism is totally outrageous. I am
beginning to understand how David formed his negative opinion
of London life. In truth, I suspect that any former student with
half a brain simply wouldn't want to become a member of such
an establishment.

After a day organising my computer and browsing through
Harrods I am well worn out and more than eager to head back
to France. Harrods is full of the most ridiculous and expensive
goods—incredible household furnishings, like cushions edged
with spangles and ostrich feathers, and clothes that are osten-
tatious, impractical and overpriced. I wander about in a daze,
wondering who buys all this crap—and indeed who can afford to
buy it. But the place is packed with credit-card waving tourists
and I can only assume they have more money than commonsense.

On my last couple of nights in England I head out of London
to stay with some of our oldest friends who live in a quaint house

in a leafy lane in Surrey. Bev is an Australian artist and fabric designer and her husband Julian, a filmmaker, worked with David on a couple of features back in Australia more than thirty years ago, and they have lived in the UK since then. Bev has always worked from home and Julian has bumbled along from one eccentric film project to another for more than twenty years. His current obsession is crop circles—those mysteriously perfect geometric patterns that appear in wheat fields in certain parts of the country, usually places of spiritual significance. Julian speaks in an amusing loud and cultured mumble, and invariably rambles on about his latest venture as though you automatically know everything about it. He breathlessly describes to me the two years he has spent putting together a documentary that purports to be 'the ultimate investigation' of this peculiar phenomenon. Having also recently discovered the joys of computer technology, he has been editing the film at home. He shows me hilarious extracts and interviews with earnest young devotees who are convinced that aliens are responsible for the midnight appearance of patterns in the fields. It is wonderful to have friends who are loony, and Julian is loonier than most. Bev and I exchange looks when Julian comes out with yet another outrageous anecdote about his crop circle exploits. The funniest angle for me is that Julian doesn't really have much faith in the commercial viability of the film, in spite of the fact that he has spent two years and a lot of his own money getting it to editing stage. I keep suggesting possible outlets—the Discovery Channel or another pay-TV station—but he shakes his head. He hopes he may be lucky enough to sell a dozen or more copies over the Internet, and I seriously wonder why he has bothered going through with the whole exercise. But that's Julian. I love him.

Anthony picks me up on the last evening and we drive south towards Portsmouth for a repeat performance of the overnight ferry. He has been attending a 'self-discovery/improvement' seminar in London over the weekend, and is as high as a kite after three days of undergoing what I consider to be mesmerising exercises in brainwashing. This moneymaking pop psychology, where groups of people are separated from the real world for a few days and put through a series of confronting workshop exercises to break down barriers and supposedly put them 'in touch with their feelings', leaves me quite cold. And Anthony knows it. He starts detailing his weekend experience from the beginning, describing every exercise, its aim and its outcome, and asks for my opinion on each. I point out that the issues they are addressing are very basic indeed. Not earth-shattering revelations, but good old-fashioned commonsense. We talk well into the night while crossing the Channel and again for most of the following day as we undertake the long drive from the coast to the southwest. He gradually comes back to earth and simultaneously the weather improves. It has been grey and raining for the six days I spent in the UK but by the time we reach the Lot the sky is brilliant blue and the sun is shining. I feel I have come home.

25

Sᴇx ɪꜱ ᴀ ᴅɪʀᴛʏ ᴡᴏʀᴅ ᴛᴏ ᴀ person living for six months in self-inflicted celibacy. In the twenty-nine years that we have been together, David and I have managed to maintain a monogamous relationship despite a couple of brushes with romance on both sides that could easily have gone the other way. We are quite proud of our achievement, though it remains largely unspoken, and neither of us suffers from that nervous insecurity that plagues couples whose relationships are under threat of imminent infidelity.

To say that sex has been an important part of our relationship is an understatement. At times it seems to me that it was the only thing that bound us together, especially during those early years when we argued so often about money or child-rearing. In the years we have been together, David has spent a lot of time absent from the house and from my bed. Indeed, for twenty years he was away for the larger part of each week in Sydney, camping overnight in his office; and of course when he was in the midst of producing a film I rarely saw him at all. This always

2 1 4

added a certain spice to our relationship. There is nothing like a passionate reunion to keep the blood pumping.

I have never been one to fritter away a lot of time contemplating sex. Like many busy women, thoughts and fantasies about sexual encounters rarely enter my head from one day or week to the next. Unlike young men who, I once read, think about the sexual act twelve times a minute, I'd be more likely to think about sex twelve times a year, and only then as a direct result of my hormonal cycle. As a younger woman my casual approach to sex was undoubtedly a result of physical and mental exhaustion. Every day of my younger life was filled with work and demanding children and deadlines and family problems and issues—for many years I simply collapsed into bed every night far too knackered to give sex a second thought. For me it was either there or it wasn't. Not a problem. David, on the other hand, was always very keen so I simply left it to him to initiate sex. It seemed to suit us both perfectly. In our earlier years together he often initiated sex in the most unlikely and sometimes uncomfortable places—in the back seat of our car coming home from the theatre, or at the bottom end of the garden late at night when the children were in bed. I suspected this was his way of gaining a little privacy for us, because of my mother living in the adjoining bedroom. Not that making love in the back seat of a car can be regarded as all that private, it was more the illicit business of spontaneous sex in a public place that obviously appealed to him. Over the past few years our sex life has dwindled a little, which I expect is perfectly normal for couples living together for such a long time. And car sex hasn't been on the cards for quite some time, fortunately. When we do get around to it, sex is still as enjoyable as ever, even if it does lack the urgency and passion of our youth. It has simply evolved into a comfortable and comforting thing!

In the months leading up to my departure for France, David and I exchange a bit of light-hearted banter about the possibility of my having a fling while so far from home for so many months. It's never a topic we discuss, as such, just a few throwaway comments and a couple of jokes about middle-aged women on their own in a foreign land. It is pretty obvious that the idea has occurred to both of us and in a way we are exploring each other's reactions, though it goes no further. During my first few months away I rarely give sex a moment's thought. I haven't come on this journey to indulge in a raging affair with a French farmer, although now I wonder if David secretly imagined that this was partly on my mind when I decided to opt out for six months.

But once I am well settled in my house in the woods and living a relatively normal day-to-day existence, the thought of sex suddenly dawns on me. And like a child who has been told that sweets have been banned for bad behaviour, I become a little obsessed by the thought of it. It's a bit like a medical diet I was once forced to follow in order to identify food allergies. While on this restrictive diet I became obsessed with the foods that were banned. I imagined them on my plate, I could smell them all around me, and I even dreamed about them at night. Now the same thing is happening to me with sex.

My dreams are suddenly filled with sweaty sexual encounters and I awake unsettled, with various body parts either erect or engorged. It's no wonder that fundamentalist religious leaders are so often caught out publicly for having illicit sex or adulterous affairs. Once sex has become forbidden fruit it somehow automatically becomes the most tantalising thing. The objects of my sexual dreams are not David, but neither are they any recognisable person that I have encountered so far. They are just men, just bodies, and try as I might to put a face to them, they remain anonymous. I have an amusing conversation with Anthony, who is quite a religious soul, about the business of sexual fantasies. Is imagining and dreaming about adultery as bad as adultery itself? He takes the view that it is not a 'sin' but proposes that having sexual dreams and fantasies is 'unhelpful' because they lead to obsession which in turn may lead to acting out the fantasies. It's a bit like the Methodist minister who preached strongly against premarital sex because it might lead to dancing. In my case it's not so much unhelpful as uncontrollable.

Suddenly I am imagining sexual possibilities in all directions. The road worker who frequently waves and winks at me as I drive past his giant asphalt rolling machine suddenly becomes my phantom lover. I imagine him turning up unexpectedly at my doorstep and sweeping me upstairs to my dark room in the loft. Jock and I often bump into this man at lunchtime at the restaurants much loved by road workers, and he always smiles and even tries speaking to me a couple times. He's tall and dark with a quintessential French moustache, and I estimate he would be in his late thirties at most. I can't realistically contemplate suddenly engaging him in a torrid affair. I cast my eye around for other possibilities, and I realise they are very few and far between. I can't imagine having it away with someone else's husband and certainly I don't fancy the idea of luring a stranger into my bed.

On the phone one Sunday afternoon I tell David a little of my dreams and fantasies, and he sounds rather nonplussed at my revelations. We normally don't have conversations about sex—it's something we do rather than talk about. Now I am teasing him, trying to draw him into the way I am feeling, and he starts to mumble and mutter in an uncomfortable fashion.

'You make me feel very nervous,' he says. 'I'm not sure that I am going to be up to your expectations of me. You've got to remember I'm not thirty-five anymore.'

I laugh out loud, then reassure him that I'm not about to start tearing his clothes off at the airport when we finally meet again. It's funny in a way to imagine him being so unsettled by me and the way I am talking. Perhaps he would rather I simply had an affair and got it out of my system. That would certainly let him off the hook.

If I *really* wanted to, of course, having an affair would be easy to organise. French men seem to have a more appreciative attitude towards older women, and instead of being invisible after the age of forty-five, as we so often are in Australia, women still seem to be objects of desire. I have even experienced a few harmless encounters with amorous men since I arrived, though nothing that I wasn't able to handle with ease. One night in the bar of the Hotel du Commerce in Villefranche I converse in a halting mishmash of English and French with a forty-something-year old man who is on a bike riding tour across the southwest. Bike riding is hugely popular in France, and during the summer months the secondary roads are packed with obsessed riders of all ages, all rippling leg muscles and facial expressions of intense concentration. This fellow in the bar is quite attractive and appears intrigued at the idea of an Australian woman living alone in a French town in the middle of nowhere. Especially one who sits in the bar at night, drinking beer. He insists on shouting me a couple of drinks and I quickly realise I am getting myself into an uncomfortable situation. Like a coward I wait until he's distracted in a conversation with the barman, then make a hasty retreat to my small, safe room.

At one of the village fêtes another charming man makes a move in my direction, placing his hand on my leg between drinks and energetic dances around the square. He, too, is quite attractive and for a moment I seriously contemplate the possibility. The atmosphere is so divine and I am feeling heady from all the wonderful food and wine. But something inside me is blocking the possibility. Not just the fact that this man is well-known to my circle of friends and an affair with him would quickly become common knowledge. Not just the fact that I am feeling rather fat and therefore reluctant for anyone—even David—to see my fleshy naked body. But something else makes it impossible for me to step over that invisible line. It's not guilt and it's certainly not a strong sense of morality. It can only be fear of the unknown. I resort, as I so often do, to humour and self-deprecation to deflect the situation.

'Now darling,' I murmur, putting my hand over his on my knee. 'You wouldn't want to have sex with a grandmother, would you?'

He laughs it off in a rather uncomfortable way, and I slide out from the seat and rejoin the dancers in a ring.

I nearly get myself into a sticky sexual situation with a couple of burly Pompiers who arrive on my doorstep one morning selling rather dreary calendars as a method of fundraising. I smile sweetly and nod that I will buy one, dashing back into the house to find my purse. Then, in my abysmal French, I try describing the suggestive calendars occasionally produced by our local bushfire brigade back in Australia—the ones with photographs of themselves naked on every page, with just a fire hat or a hose covering their malehood. Somehow I don't seem to be communicating very clearly. The word 'nudité' is being repeated and I realise they are getting very mixed signals from this woman alone in her house in the woods. I quickly thank them and virtually slam the door in their faces, mortified at my own stupidity. I really wonder what they thought I was on about, chatting about naked Australian firefighters so enthusiastically.

In truth, the thought of a full-blown love affair doesn't really thrill me much, beyond the obvious physical titillation. By their very nature, affairs of the heart involve all sorts of runaway emotions, not simply lust, and people's lives can become tragically tangled when passion turns to love and marriages fall by the wayside. The fallout is dramatic, especially for children, no matter what their age. Even though my children are fully grown and completely independent, I can just imagine how unhappy they would be if suddenly their parents' marriage dissolved. They are so comfortable with us as a couple, as the grandparents of their children, as the ones to cook the Sunday lunch where all the family gathers. I wouldn't jeopardise this for all the passionate sex in the world.

Thinking about it later I realise just how profoundly I have been affected by my father's serial infidelities and the terrible pain they caused my mother, and our entire family. I don't wish to ever make moral judgments on other people's sex lives—it's their own affair in every sense of the word. For me, having a 'harmless' fling isn't a question of morality, but one of plain commonsense. It doesn't make sense to risk ruining a solid marriage and a happy family for a good screw. The other point that occurs to me, in passing, is that it might not be good sex. It might be terrible. Wouldn't that just be the pits, working your way up to a passionate encounter which then turns out to be nothing but a profound disappointment? I'll just have to hang out until I see David again and hope he has some Viagra!

During this period of sexual confusion I come across a couple of fascinating views on middle-aged women. Germaine Greer, in the UK's *Sunday Telegraph*, has written a feature claiming that shopping has become the 'new sex' for women of a certain age. Instead of bedroom romps, women are getting their thrills and satisfaction by cruising shopping malls and spending up big on their credit cards (or better still, their husband's credit cards). I don't quite see it myself; although I love the occasional shopping afternoon it doesn't go anywhere near fulfilling my sexual desires. Then I pick up an article by a female medical writer in the *Times* expounding the new theory that women over fifty are at their most sexually powerful. Previous studies claimed that the early thirties was the age at which women reached their sexual peak, but now this lustful phase has shifted forward twenty years. Fifty-year-old women are no longer 'old' and with meno-pausal hormonal drug therapy, they still have healthy, if not excessively active libidos. That must be my problem, I conclude. I am peaking and there's not a lot I can do about it.

26

TIME IS AN ILLUSION. It either moves very slowly, like during childhood when the summer school holidays stretch ahead endlessly; or it gallops along at an alarming pace, as it does during those hectic years when your children are growing up. It seems to me only a moment ago that my little ones were dancing around my feet in the kitchen yet now, miraculously, I am a grandmother. It seems like yesterday that my own mother was sitting at the kitchen table, drinking tea and marking up the newspaper articles that she thought I should be reading, no matter how busy I was. My days never seemed quite long enough to fit in all the things I needed to accomplish—journalistic work, gardening, writing letters or simply household chores. I looked at women who did not work full time and imagined that they had the luxury of hours and hours of empty time to sit and think, to idle away. How I longed for a lack of pressure, a little breathing space. Part of my rationale in escaping for six months was to indulge myself with some precious time to think.

The down side is that too much thinking can lead to all sorts of neuroses; some people who suffer physical and mental ailments do so because they simply aren't busy enough, they have too much time to imagine all sorts of problems in their lives: at least, that is what I have always believed, probably quite arrogantly. I also tend to the view that reflection can be left until old age, and that too much agonising detracts from the actual living of one's life. I intend to use my thinking time for a little light reflection. Not navel-gazing.

In reality, my days in France fill up naturally without effort. Instead of sitting alone in a café, making a cup of tea last for an hour and staring at the passing parade, I am struggling to keep up with a diary of social engagements and excursions to new corners of the area where I am living. I barely have time for washing clothes and writing letters home. Driving the car can be good thinking time, but I always seem to be in the company of others. Walking, too, is ideal for solitary thought, and this is where I finally manage to let my mind wander back and forth over my life without restraint.

One of the things I mull over while striding through the countryside is my journey as a mother. Before I undertook this trip to France I had already reached the unhappy conclusion that I was not the world's most effective parent. I wished that I could turn back the clock and have another go at it, back to the point at which my children entered their teens. I realise in retrospect that I set out quite deliberately to be a very different type of parent to my own. I was determined, from the start, that our home would be harmonious, without all the highs and lows and histrionics that I associated with my own troubled childhood. That isn't to say that David and I didn't have our disagreements, but they were usually conducted in rooms well away from the children or in whispers in the middle of the night so my mother couldn't overhear and be upset. If we did have an argument that became a little heated it was always very much under control, without ever spiralling into the likelihood of the sort of physical anger that so terrified me. Without totally keeping a lid on emotions, I wanted to ensure that family relationships always floated along on an even keel, which I realise now was quite an unrealistic expectation.

To achieve my goal I established ways of dealing with relationships that involved humour rather than confrontation. In managing David I would send him up or tease him into cooperating with my version of the way things should be done, instead of nagging him or becoming angry or upset. He probably didn't realise that I was manipulating him, but my comedy-led strategies seemed to work brilliantly. I dealt with the children using very much the same technique. I was more inclined to laugh off their temper tantrums or defiant behaviour, and as a result our household was generally quite jolly and relaxed most of the time. I took the view that children didn't need to be lectured about the virtues of right and wrong, about good versus evil. My parents had constantly harped on the virtues of their political beliefs and by moralising they tried to establish themselves in our eyes as examples of 'right headed' individuals. My method was to lead by example instead. I rationalised that by being kind and considerate, helpful and good natured, everything would naturally flow from that. The problem is, it doesn't always—children can take advantage of a parent who is always trying to keep the peace, and who never delivers stern warnings about the rights and wrongs of life.

I also assiduously avoided putting any pressure on the children to achieve too highly, something our parents had done to us but without backing it up with any of the support and assistance needed to help us compete and succeed on a high level. My brother Dan in particular suffered as a result of my parents' tremendously high expectations of him at school. They constantly talked about him studying law or medicine, yet never really got involved with his studies or school work in any practical sense. Although naturally gifted, he ended up opting out of high school and it was many years before he returned to his studies, eventually completing a masters and doctorate in Canada, all of his own volition.

So instead of pressuring the children to be high achievers, I got thoroughly involved with all their school and sporting activities, spending years being a canteen mother, a fund raiser and an active member of the P & C, in every sense quite intentionally doing the exact reverse of my own parents. I never actively encouraged my children to underachieve, mind you, but I did minimise the idea of striving hard for success, of struggling a little to aim higher. I was quite content for them to float along through their school years, although Miriam somehow developed her own desire to achieve; by the time she reached the last years of high school she became such an obsessively diligent student that I actually tried to lure her away from her studies at night if I thought she was overdoing it, and tempt her to stop and chill out for a while. She generally ignored my pleas.

On the negative side, I always had a tendency to cover up my children's mistakes or failures in an attempt to keep them constantly happy and to prevent any kind of unpleasant 'scene'.

I sometimes even did the boys' homework so they wouldn't get into trouble at school, but only theirs, never Miriam's—she was a natural academic and quite cheerfully took care of all her own school work and study. The boys somehow were much more dependent on me for support, and I found myself constantly finishing off their school assignments and running around madly getting their research projects together so they wouldn't feel any sense of failure. The fact that their marks were often not all that great, especially with my maths being so pathetic, was not the point. They were getting the work in on time. I was reluctant to correct their spelling mistakes, lest it damage their fragile little egos, and I am now confronting the fact that I did them a grave disservice. This overprotective style of mothering I now realise simply does not prepare children for the real world.

I made all sorts of other mistakes too. I was always ready to bail my children out of trouble, to give them money when they got into debt, or make excuses for them when they made mistakes. I was completely indulgent and totally blind to their various faults and foibles. However the very worst thing that I did as a parent was to prevent David balancing my softly softly approach with a little more discipline. He was away from the household so frequently that I reasoned he had no right to appear suddenly on a Friday night and start calling the shots. I was the one doing the day-to-day management of the children, therefore I should be the one to make all the crucial decisions. I soft-soaped the issue by convincing him that he would become the family ogre if he spent all his time at home whipping the boys into line. So he backed off and let me run with it, which probably wasn't such a good idea.

I know I was great at managing babies and toddlers by giving them a lot of time and affection and satisfying all their physical needs. But teenagers are more complex. Instead of making a stand I crumbled under their new-found power. I rationalised that it was better for them to socialise at home and I allowed the house to become a nonstop party venue, especially when David was not at home. There were always stray teenagers sleeping on sofas and piles of cushions on the floor, and I turned a blind eye to a lot of the goings-on involving sex, drugs and rock 'n roll. I felt that because they were safely under my roof, with a fridge full of food and some form of parental supervision, everything was fine and dandy. At various times the children's teenage friends stayed for weeks, even months at a time. I remember David coming home one Friday night and seeing a young man with his head well inside the fridge.

'Are you actually living here, Scott?' David asked.

Startled, the spotty youth replied, 'I guess I must be.'

All these youngsters loved the warmth, the relaxed atmosphere and the abundance of good things to eat and drink in our house. They swigged their way through dozens of bottles of my homemade beer, until I stopped brewing to prevent them from getting drunk and vomiting over the back verandah every weekend. They all loved my mother—many had no relationship with their own grandmothers—and they lolled about on her bed, smoking her cigarettes and listening to her reciting Shakespeare's verse in her inimitable fashion.

My permissive attitude towards childrearing, I have subsequently read, is not at all uncommon among baby boomers, who try to keep their children as friends during their teenage years rather than maintaining any real level of discipline. Fortunately my own children emerged relatively unscathed from this haphazard parenting method, although they well might not have; sadly, many of their friends have suffered physical and mental damage from being allowed open slather during these formative years, especially in the area of drug taking. My middle son, who is now aged twenty-five, says he wishes I had been tougher with them in this respect. Now I can only agree. I am sure the next generation will bring their children up very differently.

But after thrashing myself thoroughly for my shortcomings as a parent, I can still look at my adult children with a strong sense of pride in them as young adults. They are a group of interesting individuals, all successful in their chosen endeavours, all extremely fond of each other and very close-knit and loyal as a family group. I guess, like me, they are survivors.

I also spend my walking time contemplating my mother's life and the years we spent living together. While it was greatly strained during the years of her marriage breakup and nervous breakdown, our relationship was instantly healed at the birth of my first child, a daughter. It was quite amazing how Mum's spirits lifted when Miriam arrived on the scene. Suddenly she was more positive, as if she had something to live for again. So perhaps I was fortunate to have had my first child in my early twenties, as it was the catalyst for a satisfying and long-term reconciliation with my mother.

Living in such close physical proximity to her for more than twenty years longer than most women, I really got to know and understand Mum with an intimacy that would otherwise not

have existed. She rarely got sick, but when she did I nursed her.
When I got sick, which seemed to be much more frequently, she
doted on me like a child. She dashed up to the shops and bought
lemonade, made chicken soup and tenderly checked on me
every half hour. She took over the care of the children and
seemed to revel in being totally in charge. I remember being
sick a couple of times before she arrived on the scene, and
as every mother knows, it's pretty awful being alone at home
coping with toddlers when all you want to do is crawl into bed.
Having my mother in the house made it possible for me to have
time out. We rarely had disputes about our domestic roles, yet we
never formally discussed who would do what; we both just saw
what needed to be done, and did it. Most of the time our relationship was one of easy companionship.

From time to time over the years Mum and I had deep conversations about the past, especially about all the things that went
wrong within our family. She spent a lot of time reflecting on
various events in her life that troubled her deeply. In particular
the suicide of my father's first wife Veronica, whom she never
knew, caused Mum a lot of pain; no doubt she identified strongly
with the destructive nature of my father's behaviour, and knew
how closely the situation had driven her to the brink of suicide
herself. We often had a cup of tea at the kitchen table and talked
about Veronica, how she must have felt as a young woman
alienated from her own family because of her unacceptable
marriage, and then abandoned emotionally by the man she had
obviously adored. She must have been truly desperate, knowing
she was leaving behind two young children. In those days of
course little was understood about depression, and no help was
available to her.

Mum was also haunted by the memory of my little sister Jane who died almost fifty years ago. She always remembered Jane on her birthday and on the anniversary of her death, and over the years when various of my friends had miscarriages or still-births or cot deaths, she always relived the terrible pain of losing a child: it was an unbearable agony from which she never recovered. A lot of her ongoing grief was caused by helplessness, anger and guilt. It's unthinkable now when parents are encouraged to stay in hospital with their sick children, to sleep beside them in the ward, that my mother and the women of her generation should have been so sharply dismissed from the hospitals where their children were being treated. Mum was actually told outright that mothers being present in the ward prevented the children from recovering. That children 'acted up' when their mothers were in attendance and so were more likely to remain on the sick list for longer. Parents were not consulted about treatment options, nor informed about the progress of their children's illness. Jane was in hospital for an unbelievable six months, and my mother was only able to visit a dozen times. She never really understood what was actually wrong with Jane— there had been various theories, including TB, but no definitive diagnosis was ever made. Only a week before Jane actually died, my mother had been told by the hospital that she was ready to be discharged and come home at last. My mother was incredibly excited, although daunted at the prospect of caring for a sickly child in the midst of such constant family turmoil. Then one day at 2 am a phone call came. Jane had died suddenly in her sleep. My mother took the call. Stunned, she woke my father with the news—he would have been deeply in sleep, having downed his usual half flagon of claret. Later when

Mum described his reaction she always shook her head with disbelief.

'He just grunted and said "Good", then rolled over and went back to sleep.'

I was always outraged whenever Mum retold this story, even more so when I realised that she had somehow managed to come to terms with his heartless response. I think that Jane is buried somewhere at Rookwood cemetery, without a head-stone. There would have been no money for much of a funeral, especially if my father felt so indifferent. Jane's death certificate stated that she died from pneumonia, but this was never a satis-factory explanation for Mum, who felt in her heart that her baby daughter had faded away from lack of love.

My mother's attitudes towards these tragedies in her life tended to vary according to how she was feeling when recounting the story, and how much whisky she'd had to drink at the time. When maudlin, she was more inclined to forgive my father his 'sins', and dwell only on the positive and lovable aspects of his personality. She used the tragedies as an explanation for his behaviour, a rationale for his drinking. But when she was stone cold sober her attitude was much harsher and less forgiving. These mother and daughter soul-searching sessions were quite valuable for me, a form of therapy that helped me put some of the unhappiness of my childhood where it belongs. In the past. Sadly, I don't believe Mum ever resolved the past for her own peace of mind. She still carried a lot of anger and bitterness and was never able to accept the role she played in the dramas of the tumultuous twenty-five years of her marriage.

27

THE SEASONS CHANGE ALMOST overnight. With just a few cold evenings the summer seems to be over and the days are growing shorter at a quickening rate. I am accustomed to a more gradual fading out of summer, and even though there's a brief respite with a few precious warm days, there is a chill in the air that's impossible to deny. The landscape, too, changes just as dramatically. Late summer harvesting of maize is hurried along, and the fields are quickly ploughed for the winter wheat crops. Where just a few days ago were tall stalks of green, ripening corn, suddenly there are bare fields with freshly turned, ginger-red soil that looks luscious in its fertility.

The vineyards are spectacular in their russet phase now that the harvesting of grapes is over. From an elevated position—and so many of the old fortified villages are on hillsides with fantastic views to the fields below—the varieties of grape are obvious, as each block of vines turns to a different shade of red, orange or yellow. It's a dramatically different view to that of just a few weeks ago. A patchwork again, but a completely new one that is even more beautiful, if this is possible. The woods are now golden shades of yellow and pink. There seem to be no red foliage trees, but the poplars are breathtaking in the intensity of their yellow leaves while the chestnut trees turn pink for a day or so before changing to brown and dropping their canopy. The chestnuts themselves are falling, too, and I am intrigued, never having seen them before. The circular seed pods look like some toxic Australian sea creature with sharp spikes that make them tricky and painful to pick up in my bare hand. The locals gather chestnuts for market and they well know the trees with the largest, plumpest nuts. They wait until the seed pods burst naturally and shrink back, revealing the glossy brown husks which they then collect with long, wooden tongs to avoid contact with the piercing spikes. The chestnut harvest brings the small and shy red squirrels out of the forest, and I see them scampering along the road verges gathering a storehouse for the long winter ahead. They are more endearing than the large grey squirrels that seem to have overrun the UK, and even though they are considered rare, I see half-a-dozen during the first week that the chestnuts are falling.

It's easy to imagine the farming families here feasting on wild boar and duck breasts and goose fat for generations, but that simply is not the case. It's not all that long ago that the farmers were peasants with no hunting rights in the woods, which were reserved solely for the upper classes, and so they relied on the wild chestnuts as a major source of protein. Chestnuts are still treated with some reverence. At St Caprais there is even a chestnut festival in early autumn with a community meal or repas held again in the village square, but this time inside a large white marquee because of the autumn chill. There are fewer people and no live bands thumping out music, but the atmosphere is just as jolly with the farming families gathering to dine on pork and prunes with a side serving of mashed chestnuts. It's a hearty meal, with all the usual courses—soup and salad and cheese and tart—and again so many bottles of vin rouge that I simply lose count. This time the children have decorated the tent and the tables with colourful cartoon drawings of chestnuts, each one showing considerable imagination. The chestnuts riding horseback catch my eye, along with a couple of jaunty, plump interpretations that look a bit like Jock. I can imagine my grandsons having fun drawing these comical creations.

Walnuts also ripen and fall at this time of year, although they are not wild trees but cultivated varieties that are planted as an alternative protein source. Every farm boasts four to six huge old trees, often positioned along the roadside, but such is the attitude of honesty and neighbourliness, that nobody dreams of picking up a fallen walnut unless the owner of the tree has given express permission: these crinkled brown nuts are traditionally too important to survival to be treated as simple windfalls.

A sudden windy overnight storm clears many of the walnuts from the trees and for several days I see men and women in long gumboots with baskets, stooping to harvest them. Once again the quality and size of the nuts is variable. Roger, Jock's artist friend from Loubejac knows of several trees where he has been given permission to pick up the nuts and he takes me along. The walnuts fall, carrying with them a black casing which quickly shrivels from the shell but leaves an inky stain that marks our fingers as we pluck the nuts from between the wet, fallen leaves that smother the ground. It's a back-breaking task when undertaken for several hours, but the yield is fantastic. The nuts need to be washed clean of their inky markings before being laid out on trays to dry for a week or so. Farmers who sell their walnuts, either to market or as a commercial crop, tend to bleach the shells to give them a paler appearance, but I prefer the natural dark colour of those left untreated. When I devour some of those from Roger's bountiful harvest, I realise I have never tasted truly fresh walnuts before. They have a much more intense and sweet flavour than the ones I buy each Christmas for the children to crack open on the back steps. I hunt out some recipes and experiment by making a warm walnut tart which is quite simple but also time consuming because the nuts must be cracked open and then crushed. The pastry, a pâte brisée, is extremely rich, but with the walnut and egg mix baked inside it's one of the best desserts I have ever attempted. I will make sure to try it out on the family when I get home.

The Lot is especially known for the diversity and profusion of wild mushroom species which start emerging from the tall native grasses in the woods in autumn. Villefranche is usually the centre of cèpe marketing, where barrows of these gritty, knobbly but flavourful fungi are bought and sold for several weeks from quite early in the season. This particular autumn, how-ever, is notably warm and dry and as the weeks pass people vocally lament the lack of cèpes in the woods, especially as the previous season was the biggest for decades. I, too, am a little disappointed, but Roger is determined that I will gather and eat wild fungi, even if it means searching the woods early every morning. The mushrooms supposedly spring from the soil ten or twelve days after good rains, but this autumn is without heavy falls, just the occasional light shower followed by weather that is too warm and dry to produce anything of interest.

There are literally hundreds of species of mushrooms, many of them edible but many are also highly toxic. The pharmacies have huge colourful posters on display, indicating which mushrooms are safe and which will cause serious stomach upsets— or even death—but many of the good and bad species are so similar in appearance that it would take an expert to be able to tell the difference. Luckily, Roger is an expert and he introduces me to some wild and wonderful mushrooms that look as though they'd poison an elephant but in fact have the most sublime flavour and texture. People who don't know the difference between the safe and dangerous species are advised to take any mushrooms that they gather to the pharmacy for positive identification, but in spite of this free service every season at least a couple of reckless mushroom munchers fall by the wayside.

Jock is also keen on wild mushrooms, but he is not quite as knowledgeable as Roger. Some friends give him a basketful of what they believe are common field mushrooms and he cooks them up with olive oil, butter, garlic and parsley for a late afternoon feast, then is left with a severe gutache that lasts for several days. I am a little nervous when I first contemplate eating some of the huge mushrooms I find popping up in the lawn around my small cottage, so I dash down to Lucienne's place with them so she can check them out. She assures me they are fine and their exquisite flavour convinces me she knows what she's talking about.

Roger calls me early one morning, saying he has spied 'something interesting' for me to look at in the woods. I beetle over, camera in hand, and he greets me wearing tall gumboots, a thick woollen scarf, jaunty black beret and carrying a basket over one arm. He leads me through a field and into a woodland clearing where giant parasol mushrooms are bursting from the rich, moist soil. These pale golden orbs look like the mushrooms of a child's fairy story: high on slender stems, they have perfectly rounded tops. We only need two or three to create a satisfying meal, so we gather them in the basket and Roger cooks them up for lunch accompanied by crusty bread and wine, followed by cheese. It's all rather the stuff of dreams, sitting in Roger's pretty stone cottage in deep France, sipping great wine and eating fresh wild fare from the woods, a reminder that life can really be so simple yet so divine. We repeat this ritual several times over the next month, and each foray into the surrounding woods and fields yields a different species. Shaggy inkcaps, which look fiercesome and ooze an evil-looking black liquid, are a special favourite; their flesh is rich and juicy, like fine fillets of chicken breast. And trompettes de la mort (trumpets of death) which are small jet black mushrooms that look deadly but taste quite wonderful, are completely harmless, in total contrast to their appearance and name. I can understand how everyone becomes addicted to this mushroom-hunting ritual. The training of the eye to spot the elusive fungi hiding in the long grass, the thrill of the chase, the flavour of the spoils. I am determined to come back next autumn and try again, hopefully in a more abundant season.

Autumn into winter is also the legal season for hunting, and the chasseurs, or hunters, now fill the nearby woods with the piercing sounds of gunshot, making them suddenly a dangerous place for walking, especially at the weekends. Hunting is a cult in France, and devotees are a particular breed of man (though there are also a few women) who wear jungle greens and bright fluorescent orange baseball caps which have been thoughtfully introduced to help reduce the incidence of accidental shooting. It is a topic of some amusement among the non-chasseur population, how often the hunters manage to shoot each other instead of the wild boar or deer that are their intended target. It's not a laughing matter, however, as every year unwitting walkers are killed. I am informed, as a warning, that a woman was shot in the head when out walking just a few villages from here. An eighteen-year-old boy on his first chasse was also killed. My exercise regimen goes out the window, especially when I am woken at dawn by the sound of guns blazing in the woods near the house.

On Sundays the chasseurs are out in force. They're easy to spot because most of them drive the small white vans that seem to be a symbol of testosterone-laden masculinity. The vans, which only have a front seat, are relatively cheap as well as being eligible for a government subsidy as 'farm vehicles'. There are thousands of them in southwest France, usually belting along the narrow winding roads far too fast, and more often than not on the wrong side. The chasseurs are often staked out on the edge of the woods, near the roadside, gun in hand with grim facial expressions; they honestly don't look as though they are enjoying themselves in the slightest. Even walking along the edge of the road when the chasseurs are around is perilous—if a deer suddenly breaks from the woods their guns will be swinging wildly and aiming at anything that's moving. You seldom hear one lone shot. It's always a wild volley and I am relieved not to be in close proximity when I hear the gunshot cutting the air. Adding to the danger is the chasseurs' indulgence in long lunches on Sunday, just like every other French citizen. The idea of them crashing through the woods after a three-hour lunch, vin compris, is not a happy one.

Although deer and boar are the main targets of the chasseurs, they also hunt rabbits, hare, pheasant and wild duck. Most birds in the countryside are now protected, because of the devastating impact that year-round shooting has had on wild bird populations over several centuries. Indeed, until a few years ago the sound of birdsong was rare in rural France, apart from pigeons, which breed so prolifically that they are sometimes known as airborne vermin; however, because their droppings are a valued source of soil-enriching nutrients, they have never been wiped out. Not so lucky the smaller, less flashy birds of the countryside, whose decline is explained by my regional recipe book: it features delicacies like 'woodcock on fried bread with blackberries', 'partridge with cabbage', and 'thrush casserole'. Poverty and hunger rather than greed were the cause of the small birds' decimation—indeed everything that could move was used to pad out the meagre food sources on offer. Small birds were an important source of food right up until after the Second World War. It wasn't until tractors and other more sophisticated pieces of farming equipment were introduced—bringing greater agricultural prosperity—that the situation improved. These days, greater affluence means that such drastic measures as eating our tiny feathered friends are not necessary—only the larger birds can be hunted, and then in strictly regulated numbers. It's incredible to imagine a country stripped of its bird life, but wonderful to know that numbers are increasing rapidly due to some commonsense controls.

One early autumn morning I sit on my small porch in the sun, drinking tea and admiring the view of sloping grassland, golden woods and autumnal fields. I have to go out for a few hours, and when I return it's to a scene of devastation: the grassland has been torn apart and turned upside down, with each tuft shredded into fine particles. It is a frightful mess, and I wonder what has happened here. Then it dawns on me— sangliers, or wild boars, have paid the garden a bold daytime visit, using their large black snouts and sharp tusks to rip the lawn apart in search of small grubs. I have seen them twice on the road to Cahors, once early in the morning and again at dusk. They scoot out of the scrubland and onto the road, posing the same sort of danger as kangaroos back home. The first one simply runs across my path, a fair way ahead; the second dashes out fifty metres in front of the car but is unable to mount the bank on the other side. He turns to go back but hesitates for a moment, glaring at me as the car advances towards him. Thankfully he then makes a break for it and disappears back where he came from—I can just imagine what would happen to my small car if I hit him full force. I am struck by how ugly these wild boars are, and how different from our own wild pigs which are descended from domestic ones that have gone feral. I am glad I wasn't home when the sangliars came to call!

News travels fast, and the chasseurs hear of my porcine visitation. The following Saturday morning I realise that several hunters are stalking around the woods nearby, hoping to meet my ugly friends. If wild boars taste anything like they look, I am happy to skip that particular meal. Roger, however, decides to hold a chasse dinner, consisting of wild foods either hunted or gathered from the woods. Several months previously he and Danny, quaffing a glass of wine in the dwindling twilight, spotted a hare bobbing through the fields below Roger's house.

Although it wasn't then legal hunting season, Roger took a pot shot and missed, then handed the gun to Danny who likewise took aim and bagged it in one. Having killed the poor creature they felt obliged to do something with it—so it was cleaned up, hung for a bit, then popped out of sight in the freezer. Hare is not a tender meat, and needs to be severely dealt with to make it palatable. It takes Roger several days of marinating the defrosted hare in wine and herbs to tenderise it, then he cooks it long and slow over two successive days, adding wild mushrooms and carrots for flavour. Jock, Danny and I gather at Roger's for the dinner and I have brought along a warm walnut tart because although Roger is a great cook, he is not a 'sweets' man.

We start with an aperitif of red wine laced with cassis and walnut liquor, followed by a cèpe tart with crumbly short pastry and eggs supplied by the local farmer's wife. The braised hare is accompanied by piles of crispy potatoes sautéed in goose fat and followed by salad greens from Roger's garden lightly tossed in walnut oil, then mouth-watering runny Brie cheese. The hare meat is rich, incredibly rich—just a few small cubes are quite enough to eat in one sitting, though the sauce is absolutely sublime, and we mop our plates with bread between courses. Even Jock finds it hard to eat a large portion of hare, pushing it round the plate with some effort. When you consider that the smallest book in the world is 'The List of Foods Jock Doesn't Enjoy Eating' it really means hare is an acquired taste! When we dine at Roger's we follow common French practice of using only one plate, knife and fork for the entire meal: the idea is to wipe the plate clean with bread between entrée, main course, salad and cheese. Given the number of courses these people love to eat, it makes commonsense to recycle rather than wash up mountains of dishes.

Carole tells me of a special meal prepared one evening for the hunters at Madame Murat's, using some of their catch. Forty or so strapping men descend on the restaurant at dusk for an aperitif, accompanied by only one or two wives and girlfriends. It's very much a bloke's night out, and the meal is a serious one.

A wild boar's liver, weighing at least eight kilos, is sautéed in a massive frying pan and served with garlic, parsley and a red wine sauce. Next come the boar's kidneys which have also been pan fried, and are apparently extremely rich and tasty. As if sufficient offal has not already been consumed, a third entrée is dished out—boar's testicles poached in wine with capers. Madame Murat is quite red in the face by now, but the blokes are extremely happy. The main course is the roast wild boar itself, glimmering with crispy fat and basted in its own juices. By now it's almost midnight and the party is getting rowdy, as jugs of wine are thrown back and tales of hunting exploits exchanged, but more courses and more wine are to come before Carole staggers home, well after 2 am, with the party still going strong. Heaven knows how the restaurant managed to open for lunch again the following day, or how the hunters managed to rouse themselves to stalk the woods again all weekend.

A couple of weeks into the hunting season, Jock's black tomcat Shagger disappears. The body of another similar village tom is found in Sue and Andy's garden next door, but it's not Shagger; the dead cat has what appears to be bullet holes in the side of its neck, and we can only assume Shagger has met a similar fate. It's common knowledge that bored or frustrated hunters will take a shot at anything that moves, including village cats on their hormonal rounds. Jock is greatly saddened at the loss of his scruffy old friend. The same week one of the kittens Sue brought from Spain is knocked down and killed by a car in the narrow street out the front of the house—it's the second time one of their animals has been run over in St Caprais.

Meanwhile I mysteriously acquire a ginger tom that comes screaming at me out of the night, demented with hunger, eyes blazing red in my torch beam. I wonder how on earth he has found me here in the middle of the woods, a good distance from the nearest barn or farm. Unlike Pierre and the other village cats in Villefranche, who were being fed by half-a-dozen other people, this stray will be quite a responsibility to take on because I can't just throw him out, close the door and walk away when I leave in December. But it doesn't look as though he has anywhere else to go. I name him Jacques le Roux (Jack the Redhead) and he follows me from room to room, yowling for food and generally being very demanding. It's as though he's suffering from separation anxiety, and yet I have only just met him. I force worm tablets down his throat and apply flea powder liberally from ears to tail tip, and he purrs as if it is the greatest joy of his life. He possesses all the personality of ginger cats, and I find his company very appealing. I would have preferred, however, a half-wild cat to throw the odd scrap to, rather than this limpet that has taken me on one hundred per cent.

The attitude to cats can be hard-hearted here, but I am told a story that is quite reassuring. Danny's neighbour, Monsieur Besse, has a tribe of wild barn cats, originally numbering twenty-six in all, that once belonged to his parents, both deceased some ten years. Since they died he has travelled daily from nearby

Frayssinet to feed these cats. Eventually he decided the only solution was to desex as many as possible and he set traps, catching and carting at least sixteen furious furballs to the veterinary clinic. Now they are down to only seven cats, all plump and healthy, and all still fed daily by Monsieur Besse. They run wildly to greet his car as it pulls into the farmyard every evening, rain, hail or shine. Danny also slips them the odd bowl of cat kibble, but they are still quite wild and impossible to get close enough to give them a stroke.

I seem to be a cat magnet: Jacques le Roux becomes so firmly attached that I now worry about what will happen to him when I eventually leave. Just when I was enjoying freedom from all responsibility, I now have a small creature to consider.

As the weather cools and winter approaches, the festivities of summer wind down and various members of the group peel off in other directions. Miles and Anne have long gone, as he still works full time in London and six weeks is all they can spend at their glorious summer residence. They pop down again for a week in the autumn and when we lunch together at Madame Murat's on their way to the airport at Toulouse, I know I'll not be seeing them again.

Anthony, who spent last winter camped in a makeshift house in one of his outbuildings, has vowed never to endure a winter in the Lot again without central heating. Needless to say, he hasn't quite got that far with his renovations, so he packs up his four-wheel drive and a trailerload of goods, including some boxes of fine wine, and heads back to the UK and comfortable civilisation. Andy and Sue leave for their house in Spain, with their dog and remaining kitten on board their crowded station wagon. Then Roger decides he must also return to England and close up his much-loved summer cottage for at least five months. We have several farewell dinners including one he prepares for us and one cooked for the remaining crowd by the indefatigable Lucienne.

I start feeling rather sad at the dwindling numbers, especially as I have a feeling that once I leave I shall probably never return. Life is like that. I always intend to come back but I rarely do. I know perfectly well that once I fall into my old routine of work and family and other commitments, it will be very difficult to find the time, not to mention the money, to take another holiday in this part of the world that I have grown to love so dearly. As the days get shorter I feel a certain gloom descending that makes me feel homesick for Australia and my family, yet I am reluctant to leave my present home and my new-found 'family'.

28

MY MOTHER DIED SUDDENLY four years ago. It was unusual for a woman of my generation in Australia to have her mother living under the same roof for more than two decades. Certainly it was difficult at times, and we had our fair share of serious arguments—usually about trivial issues—which could take days or even weeks to sort out.

Looking at the old farmhouses in the Lot where extended families of three or more generations all lived together in one small room—cooking, eating and sleeping, making love, giving birth and dying within four walls—reminds me strongly of how it was in our family. The expectations we now have about our quality of life and our relationships are much higher than they once were. In previous generations people 'put up' with a lot more—less than perfect marriages were common but did not automatically end in divorce. Several generations lived under the one roof if financial circumstances were stretched, and even if there were complaints and bitching, the situation was tolerated. People made an effort to get along with members of their own family, even if they found them seriously wanting. Now, of course, we expect life to be perfect, in materialistic terms, and in our personal relationships. Marriages are tossed over at the first sign of a crack, and rarely, if ever, do more than two generations co-exist. This shift has even extended into non-Anglo Australian communities which traditionally included live-in grandparents. We simply won't tolerate the inconvenience of sharing a bath-room or having to cook dinner for large numbers of people. We are too busy and probably too self-absorbed to be bothered.

Having Mum as a permanent part of our family was a gift. Her humour and intelligence filtered down the generations and added greatly to the richness of the children's lives. Mum had many passions—classical music, literature, history and politics— and she supervised all the children in their music lessons and nightly practice. They were too much in awe of her to refuse. She drummed Shakespeare into their heads, along with gram-mar and perfect pronunciation, Latin and poetry—all the things I didn't have the time or inclination or energy to introduce into their formative minds. She loved to cook and potter in the garden, she adored the animals and even liked to chop wood for the open fires before she became too frail to do so. Best of all, she was my companion during David's lengthy periods away from home, and helped provide some structure and discipline in those areas of childrearing where I was totally lax.

In the last few years of her life Mum became very dependent on us all, both physically and emotionally. She was one of those strong-minded individuals who had no time for dying, although she knocked herself around daily with excessive drinking and smoking, which contributed to her final demise. Towards the end she had some terrible falls in the evenings after drinking, and we installed railings and other safety measures to help her remain mobile. She adored spending time with the children's teenage friends and loved it when people came for dinner, especially if there was some lively debate. She swore loudly and frequently abused people if she disagreed with their opinions. She never lost her passion for controversial political standpoints, and often shouted out 'Up the Revolution' as she lurched off to bed at the end of an evening.

When Mum died, we were all taken completely by surprise, even though she had been frail for some time. Her death was heralded only by a sharp pain down one side, which she decided not to mention to anyone for at least twenty-four hours. It was typical of her to minimise any aches and pains for fear of being treated like an old crock. She was tough and could put up with terrible agony—like the gout she frequently suffered in her feet—with little or no complaint. But on this occasion the pain became too intense for her to ignore. She joked about it to her youngest grandson Ethan, 'I think I'm dying, but don't tell your mother.'

So he didn't. Eventually, however, he realised things were far from all right and he contacted me by phone. I immediately returned home. He also called our family doctor who tried valiantly to get an ambulance to take Mum to the local hospital. It was a Friday night and it was raining. There had been a couple of minor car accidents, and all the ambulances were in use. In the end I carried Mum to my car myself, climbing over a pile of bark mulch for the garden that had been delivered outside the front gate earlier in the day, her small, thin body cradled in my arms as I stumbled in the rain and the dark. The casualty department of the local hospital was a chaotic nightmare.

I insisted on Mum being given a bed to lie on, but it was a good four hours before a doctor was able to examine her. Four hours of agony she suffered, while I lay virtually on top of her, stroking her head and trying to keep her calm. Eventually she was given some pain relief and a diagnosis of kidney stones, but as the painkillers started to work she began looking gravely ill, and the diagnosis changed. There was a suspicion of something more sinister, and the medical staff decided she should fly to a larger hospital at the base of the mountains.

Mum's reaction to the suggestion of being lugged into a helicopter was typical. The air was blue with bad language, so they then decided that a standard ambulance would be more appropriate for her needs. The plan was to do a series of x-rays the following morning. I'll never really understand why I decided against riding with her in the ambulance, but being exhausted, I opted to go home and get some sleep. I never saw Mum alive again. She died shortly after getting to the second hospital, and when the call came through I was totally numb with disbelief.

We spontaneously organised a do-it-yourself home funeral with the casket on the kitchen table in true Irish tradition. The children and their friends, many of them artistic, decorated her plain plywood coffin with paintings from her life: her portrait on the lid; her favourite yellow roses; waratahs from the local bushland; the handprints of her only great-grandson Eamonn, then nearly three years old. We felt she had left in such a hurry, without saying goodbye. We were allowed to bring her body home for one last night, when we put the finishing touches to the work of art. The chickens were wrenched from their perches near midnight, and their feet dipped in coloured paint to decorate the sides of the coffin. Likewise the dog and the cats. Pages from her last reporter's notebook, which she maintained religiously on her bedside table to write down grammatical mistakes made by ABC broadcasters, were pasted between the paintings. The crossword puzzle she had completed on the morning that she died. A short list of teenagers who owed her money.

The next day friends and family gathered in the backyard. Everyone was handed a glass of champagne, and we all spoke in turn about what she had meant in our lives. The garden was filled with people, many of them young barefooted teenagers with dreadlocks and body piercings and tattoos. And dozens of women in my age group who regarded Muriel as their wise local elder. There were very few old people in her circle of friends.

Later at the cemetery when the coffin was lowered, balancing carefully on the colourfully painted lid was her final half-full glass of whisky and a half-empty packet of cigarettes. When we erected her headstone, a handsome sandstone Celtic cross, the stonemason had carved her favourite phrase 'Up the Revolution'.

Here in France I cannot help but compare the rather oddball send-off we organised for my mother with the traditionally formal funerals I see from time to time in the villages. There's always a sombre vehicle moving from church to graveyard with the villagers marching behind in quiet formation. The church bells are an important part of the service, and they seem to ring incessantly before the procession of villagers appears down the main street. One day in Villefranche, as I am drinking tea in the café, the bells begin in earnest, and I have a bird's eye view of the entire proceedings, without appearing to be eavesdropping. Instead of a hearse, the coffin is carried in a sort of dark blue delivery van with tinted windows and the mourners march four abreast behind it. On this occasion the coffin doesn't actually leave the van, which sits in waiting outside the church for more than half an hour. Only half the mourners go inside the church—the rest remain on the steps, as if keeping a vigil beside the coffin. Eventually the bells start up again and the mourners from inside lead the whole contingent back down the main street towards the cemetery. There is no talking or weeping or embracing, indeed no interchange between the mourners at all. The subdued, gloomy atmosphere is in total contrast to the boisterous celebration of my mother's longish life which prevailed despite our acute sense of loss. I know which I prefer!

Mum's death also started me thinking again about the death of my father all those years ago. I realised that I could never have felt the same closeness with my father, and therefore did not feel anything like the same level of sadness at his death. In all honesty, I had been relieved that he was no longer around to cause my mother anguish, and while at times I longed to see him or talk with him again, I really believed the world was much better off without him. The men of my father's generation had no expectations placed on them to perform as parents, except financially. They were not expected to help change nappies, bathe, feed or even play with small children, and emotional intimacy between fathers and daughters was certainly not encouraged. The fact that my father had not even lived up to his financial expectations by supporting the family on his income, and that he caused such havoc with his heavy drinking and womanising, greatly affected my view of him. On one level

I was in awe of his achievements, in particular his stature as a well-respected journalist, but on another, emotional, level I was frightened of him. His death, no matter how tragically perceived by others, was for me quite liberating.

29

WHEN YOU GO ON HOLIDAY it's not uncommon to fall in love. Often these holiday romances don't stand the test of time, and if those involved are sensible, they will have a cooling-off period to re-establish a balance in their lives before making a major commitment.

The same can be said for buying real estate. I can't begin to remember the number of times David and I have come home and announced to the rest of the family that we were definitely going to buy a property in the place where we had just been holidaying. In the first flush of our relationship we spent a lot of time visiting friends and holidaying in the Bathurst district, where we looked longingly at houses and farms and visited real estate agents. We did the same in northern NSW, the south coast, Mudgee, Cowra, southern Queensland, Norfolk Island and even on trips to visit members of David's family back in New Zealand. It must be the mere fact of being so relaxed when in holiday mode, of seeing so much beauty and potential all around and wanting to be part of it. Somehow when you are feeling rested and at one with the world in a new beautiful location it seems like a great idea to capture a piece of it for yourself. To hang on to the euphoric feelings of happiness you have when on holiday.

That's just what happens in France. For the first three or four months I experience the excitement of being in a truly foreign place, where people behave and speak very differently, and where everything appears exotic and fascinating. The antiquity of the houses and the gorgeous stonework; the cobbled streets and open markets; and the sheer weight of history oozing from every rustic back alley in every medieval township is totally enthralling.

After several months living in one place I started to get into the rhythm of life and learn the tricks of survival. How to find a parking place even in the most complex maze of narrow back streets. How to shop at the supermarket and deal with washing my clothes and getting my car repaired and communicating with the outside world. Then I came to realise, with a degree of disillusionment, that people in France are really just the same as people everywhere in the world. They have the same needs and desires and problems as people in Bathurst or Des Moines or Liverpool. They may behave a little strangely at times, but essentially they still do the shopping and take their children to school and cook the dinner and pay the mortgage. It's not an anticlimax, it's just coming back down to earth.

I can't ever escape the fact, however, that rural French communities are steeped in an atmosphere that is impossible to replicate anywhere else in the world. It's the history thing again, and the postcard-perfect beauty of the countryside and villages that constantly sets my heart soaring with joy. In all my time here I honestly haven't been inside a single ugly house. I have looked at some wonderful restorations and listened to satisfying personal accounts of buying and doing up rustic old houses. In spite of mutterings about unreliable tradespeople—the same complaints you hear anywhere in the world—the general message getting through to me is that buying an old house in the southwest of France and restoring it is definitely a fabulous idea. Well, at least that is the interpretation I have chosen to adopt.

David and I have occasionally had dreamy conversations about owning a little cottage in France or Italy, but we never seriously entertained the idea as being in any way realistic. Now that I have been here for some months, and gained an insight into house prices and the feasibility of actually buying a house, I can see that it's a dream that maybe—just maybe—is possible to achieve. On one of my regular Sunday calls I mention to David that I would like to look at some old houses, with a view perhaps to buying one. To my amazement he doesn't faint at the idea at all. In fact, he sounds reasonably encouraging. The main criteria will be price, of course. It will have to be cheap and it will have to be livable. We can both work virtually anywhere in our professions. As long as we have a phone, a computer and an email connection, we can work in any house in any country in the world. David comes to France every year for the Cannes Film Festival. He could simply go directly from the festival to our house in the southwest for a month or so, and I could join him. I can write books and magazine articles from France. And take photographs for my gardening library. It all seems achievable. And very, very exciting.

I start looking through cracks in doors and shutters of derelict, abandoned houses, of which there seem to be hundreds, both in the countryside and within almost every village and township. The gloomy interiors with huge fireplaces, stone sinks and wide timber floorboards speak to me of unimaginable romantic possibilities. Next I start noticing 'A Vendre' signs that lure me to stop and walk around, peek inside if possible, and assess the ambience. Having been lucky enough to find cheap rental accommodation twice by networking, I decide that I should spread the word around that I am interested in buying something, and see what pops up. Nothing much happens.

First up, Danny shows me a tiny stone house at the back of a field behind his property that his farming neighbour is prepared to sell for a song—but it doesn't have water or electricity connected, both of which can be an expensive proposition. He also knows of a similar cottage near St Caprais, which we walk to through woodland to find it packed with bales of straw. It is charming but derelict.

I half-heartedly look in the windows of local immobiliers (real estate agents) and see some wonderful-looking houses and chateaux that are way, way out of my class. Several weeks pass with no activity, then I plunge in and make an appointment to view the property books of a couple of English agents at nearby Les Arques. I have been told by friends that good cheap houses are now few and far between, but this is not what I see when I start leafing through the brochures. Dozens of old stone houses in need of love and attention smile out at me, and I make a short list of ten possibilities to inspect.

The reason so many houses lie empty for decades in this part of France is perplexing to an outsider. French inheritance laws are Napoleonic, and so complex that many houses and farm buildings are caught up in family disputes because no mutual agreement can ever be reached. In French law children are favoured over the surviving spouse, which means effectively that many widows face eviction. Even parents, if they are still alive, are further up the line in the inheritance stakes than a wife. Before an inherited property can be sold, all parties must be in agreement and if there is a falling out between them the whole matter might just be relegated to the 'too hard' basket. Added to this is the exodus of the younger generations to more densely populated regions—Toulouse, Marseilles, Paris and even London. Often elderly family members will hold onto vacant farm buildings in the hope that their grandchildren may one day take an interest, and perhaps even return to the land of their ancestors. Sadly, it's unlikely that this will ever happen, so the houses and barns, chateaux and grand residences remain empty and crumble down through decades of neglect. It's heartbreaking to see them.

From the moment I start exploring inside these vacant farm cottages and village houses my imagination plays havoc with my good commonsense. I am trying to keep my feet planted firmly on the ground, but I can't help being a little carried away in my quest to find the perfect house in the perfect setting. I am also feeling a sense of urgency as my time here is rapidly running out. If I don't find a suitable house in the next few weeks it will be too late, I will be on the plane, on the way home, probably never to return.

The first house I view formally is near Frayssinet-le-Gélat, quite close to a busy road. Set high up on a sloping acre of meadow and walnut trees, it is the typical rural basic stone rectangle with tile roof. Structurally sound, only one of the three potential levels has ever been lived in. Most French farming families lived, ate and slept in one room with very little furniture; they sat around a wooden table on wooden chairs until bedtime, then retired to timber beds somewhere between a standard single and a double in size. In this particular house the one room has been divided into four cramped living spaces, a kitchen/dining room, two bedrooms and a basic bathroom, which is more than most old French farmhouses boast—none of the houses I subsequently visit has the benefit of a bathroom. I guess it was potties and buckets sloshed into holes dug in the fields; quick forays into the woods during warm weather and strained relationships in the winter. Beneath the main central floor is a large open 'cave' or cellar, though it has possibly also once been a barn for animals. This has a dirt floor but plenty of ceiling height and potential as a living level. There is also enough space in the ceiling for more rooms in the attic, possibly a couple of small bedrooms, plus a small barn which also has potential as an extra bedroom or guest accommodation.

My initial reaction is that the house inside lacks charm and 'features'. Where are the fireplace and stone sink that I love to see in every old house? On close inspection I uncover the fireplace, still intact, hidden behind flimsy doors that have converted it into a storage cupboard. The stone sink is still there too, buried beneath some modern kitchen paraphernalia. The agent, Alice, has struggled with a maze of keys to get us inside, and just when I am feeling that it is all too claustrophobic, she throws open the shutters and reveals the view. Gasp! A wild meadow and woodland surrounds the house, and even though the road is nearby, the effect is enchanting. I want to buy it immediately. However I am booked to see eight more houses on Monday.

Patience.

Monday arrives and it's pouring with rain. A good time to see houses, because you get to assess them at their most dreary and unromantic. Our first house is near Gindou and it's a farming complex of four buildings plus four acres of meadow and woodland. The owner, a woman in her sixties driving a white van, wearing a blue pinnie and accompanied by a gangly wet hunting dog, lets us into the house. She has inherited it from her uncle and it has been empty for a long time. From the exterior the house is square and boxy with a set of stairs leading to a stone verandah and front door. The main room has the ubiquitous walk-in-fireplace, this time with a prominent gunrack over the mantel, plus a large stone sink. Once again the shutters open to reveal an enchanting view of autumnal scenery. There are two large bedrooms, each with a fireplace, winding stairs to an empty attic, and a spacious cave that could easily be converted into two large rooms. This is a more formal house, obviously owned by wealthier farmers than the average, as reflected in the outbuildings: one barn has a stone bread oven but is dilapidated, while the main barn is vast—as large as a small cathedral—with arching timber roof supports and tiles that allow shafts of light to penetrate. In the middle is an enormous cart laden high with pumpkins of every size, shape and colour. It's as if it's been art directed for a movie shoot. This huge barn has equally huge stables beneath the main floor, complete with cow bales and pens for pigs and other animals. I want it, of course. But the cost of converting this property into a comfortable house would be astronomical—it's just so huge that the materials alone would cost a fortune.

Next we wind through country lanes to a small, crumbling village that is one of the first really untidy places I have seen on my travels in France. Generally farms and their surrounds are neat as a pin, with trimmed verges and meadows kept tidy by haymaking or grazing. This conglomeration of dwellings is ancient and many of the buildings are in complete ruins, having been robbed of their stone for other construction purposes. There is evidence of some half-hearted attempts at restoration, but it all looks very down-at-heel and some buildings are quite ugly. The house we view is again enormous, a vast rectangle with elegant windows and views to golden countryside past a bubbling stream. I close my eyes and imagine how divine it would look if you could somehow block out the neighbours. But the place is a ruin, with roof tiles that must have been damaged during the wild storm that savaged France the previous January. Water has been cascading in and timbers everywhere are rotted and crumbling away. I can't believe anyone would allow this gracious old house to get into this pathetic state, but I suppose it is often possible. There's plenty of space to make a rambling family home within the four stone walls, it will just cost a small fortune to do it. The property also has a barn which is twice as large as the house but is not on the same piece of ground; it is across a small square and attached to other buildings. Separated buildings under one ownership is not uncommon, and many farms consist of tracts of land that can be kilometres apart. Again I see great potential for development but feel quite over-whelmed at what it could all cost.

The next property makes me go weak at the knees. I am defi-nitely in love. Less than a kilometre from the thirteenth-century village of Marminiac, it has two buildings abutting a narrow, winding country road. The largest building is the barn. In excellent condition, it is not too large for conversion to a comfortable living space. The farmer showing us the property has a curious handshake with two fingers tucked into his palm. I look closely to see if the fingers are damaged or missing, but no, and when not shaking hands his fingers are quite normal. He looks about eighty and he says that the farmhouse belonged to his grandparents, the last of whom died in 1932, and it has literally remained empty and shuttered for nearly seventy years. Instead of the usual doorway there is an archway with the numbers 1 and 7 carved in the lintel stone. The other two numbers have worn away, but it seems that the little house was constructed in the early eighteenth century. The roof is low but still has a steep pitch, in classic Quercy style, and although the original stone roof has been replaced with tiles, it still looks ancient. The heavy timber front door swings open to reveal a dark interior—thank heavens I brought my torch—and this is where I become totally smitten. The floor is pise, rounded stones set into the compacted soil in decorative patterns. The fireplace is huge and a ladder to the attic reveals a large enough space to make a second storey with ease. There is also a small single-storey barn adjoining the house that could easily become a kitchen and dining area.

Why is it when you see a house you love you immediately start mentally planning how it will look when restored? My mind is already racing wildly with the possibilities. This house has no water and no electricity connected and it has certainly never had a bathroom. I look more closely and notice one corner of the small barn that is falling away and a large gap between the roof and the chimney, as if the entire roof line has shifted.

Mere details. Trifles. The cottage personifies my dream

of living in France, and the fact that it also has eleven acres of woodland and fields and is quite expensive doesn't in any way dampen my enthusiasm.

My main problem now is going to be David. How can I convince him that buying a crumbling costly farmhouse on the other side of the world is a fantastic idea? I phone him at work and he sounds less than enthusiastic. I use every lyrical phrase at my disposal to accentuate the glories of the Marminiac farm. He goes quiet on the other end of the line.

'What's the bathroom like?' he finally inquires.

'It doesn't have one.'

'No bathroom? What happened to it?'

'It never had one in the first place.'

'It must at least have a toilet.'

'No, no toilet.'

'Where did they shit, for Christ's sake?'

'In the woods, I guess. It doesn't really matter. We can put in a bathroom.'

Silence.

'Isn't there one with a bathroom?' he finally asks pathetically.

'I suppose I can find one if I look around more. Can I keep looking? Can we afford it?'

'The answer is yes and no. Keep looking. We can't really afford it, but if you really, really want a place and it isn't too expensive, we can think about it.'

I start telling all my friends the fantastic news. I am going to buy a house. Become a local. Come back every year. Maybe spend six or twelve months here at a time. Learn to speak French properly. Write another book. Make a documentary. I don't know. I just know I can do it.

Margaret Barwick is a little sceptical. She has seen dozens of visitors go through the same house lust before, and apart from Jock and the Greifs, no-one has ever persisted.

'You'll just go home at the end of the six months and get busy again and never come back,' she says. 'You'll forget all about us in no time. It will just be a happy memory.'

This makes me more determined than ever. I decide to bid on the house outside Frayssinet, the one I first inspected, even though it's on the wrong side of the hill and spends most of the day in the shade. At least it has a bathroom. But my hesitation has proven fatal: the owners have accepted another bid on the house, and under French law gazumping is definitely out of the question. My offer is a little higher and the English owners are furious. They want to go with my bid, but it simply can't be done without all sorts of legal ramifications.

Despondent, I start again, but don't get very far. Where only a short while back I saw countless possibilities, David's insistence on a rock bottom price and a working bathroom have now severely limited the options. I also start to make a few enquires about the practicalities of being a foreigner owning a house in the French countryside. Anthony lends me two useful guide books on buying real estate and living in France. There are no legal constraints, however we can only spend three months at a time here unless we go through a hell of a lot of bureaucratic red tape. According to the guides, house renovations invariably cost much more than first anticipated, and can also easily rocket out of control unless you are around to supervise the work. Language difficulties, unreliable tradespeople, ongoing taxes and charges. It's all sounding very complex. There's also the issue of how much we will realistically be able to use the house, and if we will be able to rent it out when we are not in residence.

I am beginning to think that buying a house is not such a fantastic idea after all.

30

IN BED AT NIGHT I lie awake, tossing and turning and worrying into the small hours. During this entire time away from home I have slept soundly, and never had a restless night of anxiety. Now I am torn between this fantasy of living in France and the reality of my situation. I must be totally mad, wanting to buy a house on the other side of the world. My home is Australia. It's where my entire family lives, it's where I work and where my heart truly lies.

But I simply can't let go of the past six months. I have become so attached to every aspect of this small corner of the world—the fields and woods, the villages and towns, the people and the food. How can I simply walk away and carry it only as a happy memory? Somehow I must grab a little bit of it and hold onto it like mad, no matter what. During the daylight hours while I am engrossed in house-hunting, phoning David in Australia to discuss each possibility, or dragging my friends along to view a property and to get their opinions, it all seems like a splendid idea. But at night, on my own, I am racked with doubts.

I phone Miriam one evening to describe some of the amazing houses I have been seeing. I would love her to share in my excitement, because I am hoping that in time she, Rick and the little boys will be able to come to France and enjoy all the things that I love about this place. She sounds very down and when I ask her why, she bursts into tears.

'I'm bloody well pregnant,' she sobs. 'I can't believe it, but I am.'

I refrain from asking her what went wrong. I know that there has been talk about Rick having a vasectomy, and that they have been using alternative methods of contraception in the meantime. Having a fourth baby will really alter their plans, not to mention stretch their finances to the limit. Miriam has been accepted to start a postgraduate law degree next year, and the idea was that I would help a couple of days a week with the boys so she could study and complete assignments. With a new baby on the way, the plan will have to be shelved for a couple of years at least.

Miriam's news adds to my confusion. What the hell am I thinking about, buying a house in the northern hemisphere when I will now have six grandchildren in Australia? I should really put such thoughts out of my mind.

Two days later Miriam calls, and her voice sounds very different.

'It's okay, Mum. I'm over the shock and used to the idea of the baby now. Rick and I are excited about it. It will be wonderful.'

I am excited too. Another baby, and perhaps a daughter for her. I start to feel a little less anxious and continue looking half-heartedly at houses.

His film nearly finished, David suddenly decides to come to

France for the last two weeks before Christmas. A symbolic gesture, to fetch me home to the family, and to help make, I hope, a final decision on buying a house. I am still holding out some hopes for the Frayssinet cottage which has failed to pass the termite inspection: this means that the owner must now renegotiate with the prospective buyer. There is a slim chance that the deal may fall through and allow me an opportunity to pounce with a counter offer. That is, of course, if I am prepared to take on a house that is riddled with chewing insects! In the meantime I keep looking at more crumbling ruins, feeling that the whole idea of buying a house is slowly slipping through my fingers.

Although I have been accustomed to long separations from David during our thirty-year relationship, I feel as excited as a nervous teenager at the prospect of seeing him again. I wonder what he will think of my extra curves? I have managed through walking and sensible eating to shed a couple of the kilos gained during my early eating and drinking exuberance, but am still carrying quite a few extra layers around the middle. He probably won't even notice. I clean the house and light the fires because it's now well into winter and suddenly very cold. I am to meet him at the Gourdon railway station thirty minutes from Pomarède in the early afternoon. He arrives in Paris from Sydney earlier in the morning then transfers to the southbound train, so he will undoubtedly be exhausted.

He emerges messily from the last carriage, manhandling far too much luggage as usual, and I gallop along the platform to meet him, sobbing with joy at our reunion. It does seem unlikely at this stage of our relationship—tears and passionate hugs on a French country railway station. But we are genuinely thrilled to see each other again.

I have made up a double bed in the living room so we can snuggle in together in front of the fireplace. The upstairs room, with no windows, is just too cold and dark and dreary for the purposes of our reunion. The size of the bed downstairs is laughable compared to our own at home—French doubles are not much larger than a standard single bed—we will be sleeping very closely together indeed. David is by no means a small man, so if my feet are hanging over the end, and they are, his will be practically dangling on the floor.

When we finally make it into the bed, after a lightning tour of the local villages while talking ten to the dozen, it's the feeling of his familiar body against me that gives me such great pleasure. I can't help but cry a little, of course, at the joy of making love after such a long time, but it's the comfort of skin to skin contact that I have really been craving. We lie together like that for hours and hours, and almost feel reluctant to go back out into the cold to meet people and look at houses.

The next few days are exhausting. At lunches and dinners I introduce David around to my new French friends and to those members of the expatriate community who remain in the southwest for the winter. So many of them have already gone to warmer climates that he's really meeting the bare bones of the group, the stayers and the permanent residents. With typical generosity, they all host dinner parties and lunches in his honour, but for me it feels very odd suddenly having a man with me after six months' complete independence, being defined only by who I am, rather than whom I am married to. David also feels strange, coming into my intimate social circle and meeting people who I am obviously close to, but who have to him only been names in my conversations. He feels disoriented and is obviously still jetlagged because after two or three days he can't keep up the pace of eating and talking till the wee hours.

'I can't believe you have been doing this for six months,' he groans as we set out on yet another social engagement.

There is also a sense that David is coming to France to take me home. That his arrival means the beginning of the end of all the good times we have been having together over the summer and autumn. He feels this strongly too, and worries if he will be perceived as the ogre, the spoiler of everybody's fun. However the warmth of the welcome extended by my new family eases this feeling of insecurity. He will never really feel the same bond I feel with this place and these people, but he will love every moment of being here in the future. I feel totally confident.

With Alice the agent I show him over the short list of houses on offer. None of them excites his imagination. He likes the look of the Frayssinet cottage, which I show him from the road, but it is still just out of our reach.

In desperation we approach another immobiliers in Prayssac. I have been loyally sticking to my English contacts, mainly I suppose because of my language difficulties. In the window we see a property at Cazals that looks quite promising, and ask if we can see over it. The Prayssac agent, Pierre, speaks only French but tells us that he has an English woman in the agency who will be back after lunch. When we meet Liz and explain our situation, she quickly makes up a list of six or eight possible properties. Pierre takes us through the Cazals house, which is in fact two adjoining houses, one habitable and one derelict, later in the day. We take Anthony along for a second, more experienced opinion. The renovated house is small but has lots of French features and a workable bathroom and kitchen. We don't have keys to the second part of the property, but peer through dusty windows to see a large room with a beautiful stone fireplace. We love it, and Anthony nods in approval, though he points out that it doesn't have a garden of any description. Nowhere to sit out in the summer, but it's cheap and picturesque with potential to be made gorgeous. And Cazals is a wonderful ancient town with a beautiful village square and lovely shops and restaurants. This is it! We agree on the asking price, without even making a lower offer, and Pierre says he will contact the elderly owners who live just a few doors up the road.

David and I finally have an evening alone in the cottage in the woods, snuggled up by the open fire eating a simple meal that doesn't require endurance to digest. David is greatly taken with Jacques le Roux, who hasn't shown any signs of departing since he first landed on my doorstep. Jock has said he will take Jacques at a pinch, but I am concerned about his survival in St Caprais where so many cats are either run over or targeted by hunters. I can't just close up the house and abandon Jacques to his fate. We could take him back to Australia, of course, but would a French country cat ever feel at home in the Blue Mountains? The quarantine period is four months, and then there are our own cats to consider. It's a real problem.

The following morning Liz calls with frustrating news. The owners have phoned their son in Paris and he has changed his mind about the property being sold. He will inherit the two small houses one day and keeps vacillating about whether or not he really wants them. Apparently this is the third time the houses have been on the market and then withdrawn when a firm offer has been made. Pierre and Liz are furious, not just because of our obvious disappointment, but because of the waste of their time and money. Apparently this is not unusual in France. The owners want to test the market, to see how much someone is prepared to pay for their property. Then they withdraw it when a keen buyer appears. We feel angry and totally desperate because we now have only eight days before our flight back to Australia.

Liz produces a new list of properties, although a majority are further from the villages for which I have indicated a preference. We set off early the following day to look at what's on offer. The first one is at Martignac, on the other side of the Lot River, past a wild gypsy encampment that is littered with debris. It's a small village without shops but with a lovely church. The house is structurally sound but in a sadly rundown condition. The views from the windows are rather uninspiring, but it's cheap and has lots of potential if a good deal of money is spent. The second property is huge and beautiful but we don't have keys to get in. It's at Duravel, which is a township but half an hour from St Caprais and that is a real concern for me, because all of my connections are in the vicinity of Jock's village. Will I feel like a long drive home after dinner with friends? Probably not, although again this property is within our limited budget and has great potential for restoration. The other main downside is that it's smack bang beside an ugly car repair yard, which is probably why it has been on the market for several years. We move on.

The third house is in Frayssinet-le-Gélat which is right in the centre of the action as far as all my friendships and contacts are concerned. Five minutes from St Caprais. Five minutes from

Pomarède. It's where Claude lives permanently and where Miles and Anne have their summer house. Perfect. The property in question is a typical two-storey village house, with the front doors and windows opening right onto the road. I had determined not to buy a property next to noisy traffic, but we are running out of options. The house is bathed in sunlight and looks very solid, but has a crumbling layer of crépi on the outside that will need to be chipped off. It has a courtyard garden at the back and also a barn that looks large enough for conversion to a studio, or perhaps a couple of extra bedrooms. Inside the house immediately speaks to us, although we dare not sound too enthusiastic lest we are in for yet another disappointment. The main room is huge, with a wonderful fireplace that has been fitted with a slow combustion stove that serves as both central heating and as an open fire. Some of the walls are warm, cream exposed stone while others are lined with plaster, and the floors are attractive polished timber. The house is owned by an English man who has been using it as a summer residence for many years, but he is now too frail to make the journey to France. It contains simple but comfortable furniture which is all part of the purchase price—a fridge and a washing machine, a vacuum cleaner and a well-equipped kitchen. Up a handsome flight of curved timber stairs to the second floor there are two large, fully-furnished bedrooms. Unlike so many of the houses we have seen, this one hasn't been invaded by owls who have splattered the floors with their guano, the roof isn't leaking water down the walls, and the windows are intact. You could move into this small village house tomorrow and be warm and dry and comfortable. I can tell by his body language that David is excited, and we go into a small huddle. Let's do it.

Liz calls the owner in London who immediately accepts our offer. In haste the papers are drawn up, we send for funds from Australia, and we sign a preliminary but totally binding agreement with a notary at Cazals just two days before our departure. In some ways the house is a compromise, being so close to a main road, but it qualifies on every other level and we decide that we absolutely love it. We are given the keys and are able to show friends around, who congratulate us on our good fortune in finding a well-located house, in good condition, for such a ridiculously low price. We light the fire, open a bottle of good wine, and toast our future as part-time French villagers.

Next morning Alice calls to say the other house at Frayssinet, the first one I saw with the large garden, is now available. The owners have managed to extricate themselves from the contract with the other buyer. I don't believe it. We have signed for the village house, and nothing further can be done. However David and I decide that things have actually worked out for the best, as they so often do in these situations. The village house is much less expensive, so we will have more money for new furniture and renovations. It requires a lot less work, is bathed all day in sunlight, and living in a village will offer many compensations. We can walk to the bar or for lunch at the Plan d'Eau. We can get to know our neighbours more readily, which will help improve our language skills. All in all, we have come out on top!

We realise that if we are to be coming back to France every year we will need a car. I phone Richard who lent us the Peugeot and ask about his plans for the vehicle after I leave.

'Oh I'll just sell it off as quickly as possible,' he says, delighted that I haven't managed to wreck it during my six months of erratic driving.

'We'll buy it, if it's not too expensive,' I say with glee, because I have really come to appreciate its reliability and low cost of maintenance. Danny offers to store the car in his barn while we are back in Australia. This means someone can come to meet us at the train station in our own vehicle every year when we return. It's ideal.

A couple of days before we leave for home our neighbour Hugues comes to dinner with several of our other French friends. He spies Jacques curled up by the open fire, and swears he is the spitting image of his own much-loved ginger tomcat. I explain my dilemma of finding a safe home for poor Jacques, who has become so dependant on the warmth and food provided at the little house in the woods. Hugues looks delighted. His elderly parents, who live at a nearby farm, recently lost their cat who was nearly twenty years old. Although still in mourning they would love a replacement, but definitely not a little kitten. It seems too good to be true. The following night I wrap Jacques in an old blanket, with his head poking out like a baby's face from a shawl. We load the boot of the car with tins of cat food and Hugues leads us down various winding lanes to his parents' farmhouse door. They have made up a basket for him by the fire, but while we sit and drink an aperitif, thanking them profusely for adopting our stray cat, Jacques finds his way to one of the bedrooms. By the time we leave he is curled up, purring and looking absolutely at home.

Our friends combine to throw a farewell dinner for us at Claude's lovely house. No expense has been spared with the finest of foods and wines and everybody contributing to the table. David is presented with a floppy black Basque beret, which suits him to perfection, and a huge baguette to tuck under his arm. He couldn't look more like a local. My gift has been painted by the Barwicks' clever daughter Jan. It's a wonderful landscape of the southwest, with every detail included. The geese and ducks and wild boars, the village houses and walnut trees and mushrooms in the woods. There in the middle on a picnic rug are David and I, he carving the bread and me clutching a huge bottle of red wine. It's a perfect memento. I am also ceremoniously presented with my own blue pinafore, now that I am to become a real French country housewife. Wearing it I look as comfortable as any of the hundreds of women I have seen watering their geraniums or sweeping the front step.

The following morning we pack up the house in the woods and are driven to the railway station by Jan and Philippe. It's very, very hard to say goodbye.

31

IT'S ALWAYS THE SMELL of Australia that hits me when I have been away. This is the longest I have ever been away from my homeland and it's more acute. The air seems thick with the smell of eucalyptus as I emerge from the airport, even in polluted Sydney.

As we have arrived late in the evening, David and I decide to stay overnight in town so that the little ones will be awake when we get back to our house in the mountains. Aaron drives down to pick us up quite early, and he greets me in his usual offhand manner. As if I've been on a two-week film shoot rather than away for nearly seven months in another country.

'Gidday sheila,' he says with a grin, knowing that I am not particularly fond of this term of endearment.

There's something very different in my relationship with my sons. I know that they love me dearly—their wives and girlfriends often tell me so—but they are less inclined to show their feelings in any way. Aaron in particular. He doesn't even ask me about France or about how I am feeling. Nothing has changed.

On the drive home I feel quite sick to the stomach with excitement at the prospect of seeing everyone again. The journey can't be fast enough for me, I'm itching to get my hands on those little boys and to greet Ella Mary for the first time. There's no-one at the gate but I can hear the children playing in the back garden. I sneak into the kitchen, where tea is being made, and there are screams of delight. And many, many tears. It's overwhelming and quite wonderful.

I go outside and see the children, who have been well prepared for this moment. They all run to me, even little Theo who only had his second birthday while I was away. I was worried he may feel shy, and not really remember me clearly. Six months is a long time in the life of a two-year-old. But Miriam has kept my photo on the front of her fridge at the children's eye level, and apparently I have been discussed often. He falls into my arms as though he is totally familiar and at ease with my presence. Then the baby is handed to me and I feel I have really come home at last.

Next I do what I enjoy doing most. I cook up a big lunch for everyone, set the table and we gather as a family again for the first time in so many months. It all feels so familiar and comfortable and warm that instead of feeling strange, I feel as though I have never really been away. And in some respects I haven't. Not in my heart. It was just my body that was leaping around southwest France like a lunatic.

As I look around the table I see the faces of my children and their partners, laughing and talking and keeping the little ones in order. They all look so grown up and confident and sure of themselves, much more like my contemporaries than my offspring. It's difficult to imagine them as the babies and toddlers and teenagers who kept me so frantically busy for nearly three decades. I wonder to myself why they have all launched into such serious relationships at comparatively early ages. Even Ethan, the youngest by five years, has been living with the same partner, Lynne, for more than three years and they are excitedly telling us all about their plans to visit France together the following year. Of course there will be a house and car, and Ethan would love to get stuck into some of the much-needed renovations, but they will have to save their own fares and spending money. David certainly looks pleased that we are both home again, and even the noise and chaos of the five little children doesn't seem to faze him.

It dawns on me that no matter where I am in the world, I will be surrounded by people and laughter and food and wine at gatherings such as this. I may have run away with the idea of being alone. But that was never going to happen.

FOUR MONTHS AFTER I returned to Australia David Barwick lost his
long battle with cancer. Our youngest son Ethan and his partner
Lynne went to Frayssinet-le-Gélat in May to start restoring the
village house, and promptly found themselves pregnant. In June
the same year Miriam gave birth to Augustus James, her fourth
son.